VIETNAMESE COOKBOOK

Delicious Quick and Easy Vietnamese Meals Vietnamese Cookbook Recipes

(Authentic Vietnamese Street Food Made at Home)

Jack Thomson

Published by Alex Howard

© **Jack Thomson**

All Rights Reserved

Vietnamese Cookbook: Delicious Quick and Easy Vietnamese Meals Vietnamese Cookbook Recipes (Authentic Vietnamese Street Food Made at Home)

ISBN 978-1-990169-39-7

All rights reserved. No part of this guide may be reproduced in any form without permission in writing from the publisher except in the case of brief quotations embodied in critical articles or reviews.

Legal & Disclaimer

The information contained in this book is not designed to replace or take the place of any form of medicine or professional medical advice. The information in this book has been provided for educational and entertainment purposes only.

The information contained in this book has been compiled from sources deemed reliable, and it is accurate to the best of the Author's knowledge; however, the Author cannot guarantee its accuracy and validity and cannot be held liable for any errors or omissions. Changes are periodically made to this book. You must consult your doctor or get professional medical advice before using any of the suggested remedies, techniques, or information in this book.

Table of contents

PART 1 1

INTRODUCTION 2

    MEANINGFUL AND ESSENTIAL ELEMENTS 8

    'TÁM' RICE 11

    CLIMATE 12

    LIGHT AND SUBTLE 12

    SPECIAL INGREDIENTS 13

    FERMENTED SOYBEANS (TƯƠNG BẦN) 13

    SPICY AND BOLD 14

    IMPERIAL CUISINE 14

    ICONIC DISHES 14

    SWEET AND RICH 16

    SEAFOOD AND FERMENTED ANCHOVY SAUCES 16

    ICONIC DISHES: 18

ON BEVERAGE PAIRING 28

HERBS & VEGETABLES 38

    HERBS 38

    VEGETABLES 55

    DRIED SPICES 66

PART 2 118

INTRODUCTION 119

    RICE VERMICELLI WITH CHICKEN 120

    VIETNAMESE LEMONGRASS CURRY CHICKEN 123

Beef Meatball Pho 125

Vietnamese Grilled Snapper 129

Crispy Vietnamese And Pancakes 132

Vietnamese Summer Rolls 134

Vietnamese Pork Chops 137

Vietnamese Vegetarian Curry Soup 139

Vietnamese Braised Pork With Noodles 142

Roasted Shrimp Sausage Rolls 146

Vietnamese Long Bean Salad 148

Shrimp And Mango Salad 150

Vietnamese Grilled Lemongrass Shrimp And Noodles 153

Caramel Catfish 156

Green Papaya Salad 159

Chicken Papaya Salad 162

Vietnamese Butternut Squash And Salmon Porridge 165

Vietnamese Thit Bo Xao Dau 168

Vietnamese Saigon Chicken Salad 170

Rib Bun Soup 174

Vietnamese Fried Chicken Thighs 178

Vietnamese Gold Chicken Wings 181

Vietnamese Chicken Noodle Soup 183

Pineapple Shrimp Banh Mi 187

Stir Fried Beef Bun Salad 190

CONCLUSION 193

Part 1

Introduction

As a very young girl growing up in Vietnam's capital city, Hanoi, I would watch with fascination - and even rapture - as my grandmother made culinary magic in the kitchen of a local high school. I remember my family lived inside the area of a local school where my mother worked as a teacher. During the disruption and hardships of The War in Vietnam, my grandmother stayed at home and looked after my family, cooking for us every day. She also helped our family's finances by cooking foods and selling them to students of this school. It was there that I would watch my grandma cooking a mixture of traditional and inventive dishes that were adored by the students there. By cleverly overcoming the many food shortages that still afflicted the Vietnamese economy, she would conjure up wonderfully tasty and satisfying platefuls of sticky steamed rice with peanuts and mung beans that were always a huge hit with the students. Using simple ingredients, she was not only earning an income for our family; my grandma was also feeding the young of a hungry nation.

Like many talented Vietnamese housewives at that time, she'd become amazingly resourceful by drawing on unconventional food sources. Traditionally, most Vietnamese cooks would simply throw away fish stomachs, but she managed to combine this unloved ingredient with plentiful and easy-to-grow herbs and spices, thereby transforming it into the centrepiece of a truly delicious dish. Likewise, snails that she found crawling in the school grounds were harvested and turned into a meaty, succulent enhancement for one of her much-loved stir-fries. The French colonial authorities that were still governing Vietnam when my Grandma herself was young would no doubt have greatly appreciated her beautiful, creative, and economical take on one of their own distinctive national favourites.

The skill, dedication, and effort of Vietnamese home-makers of my Grandmother's generation was, and has remained, a source of great pride and inspiration to me. At a time of great adversity, these women made significant personal sacrifices - often putting their own career ambitions on hold to ensure that their husbands, children, and grandchildren would have satisfying, nutritious, and delicious meals. To me, their energy, determination, and generosity make them the great mainstays and unsung heroines of Vietnam's long-running campaigns for national self-determination and independence.

It is their spirit of invention that I want to celebrate in the dishes that I make in my own kitchen today. In every one of my recipes, I try to preserve the best of Vietnam's authentic culinary accomplishments while honouring the extraordinary creative ingenuity of cooks who have helped to establish Vietnamese gastronomy as one of the most popular in the world.

In writing this book, I owe an incalculable debt of gratitude not only to Grandma, but to my great friend and sister Ly Van. Her understanding, appreciation and insight into our shared nation's home cooking has guided me throughout my own personal journey of Vietnamese culinary discovery. I hope that the recipes that I present in this book will be just as inspiring to my readers as Ly Van's wise guidance has been to me.

Understanding Viet Cuisine

When I am exposed to a foreign cuisine, for example Western cuisine, I often have a feeling of reluctance. I don't understand the story behind it. Thus, I am scared of trying to make it, even just as a learning experience.

People from other countries love Vietnamese food, but they also get scared because they don't know how to make it like a native Vietnamese. A British friend asked me things like, "It seems Vietnamese food is spicy, isn't it?" and "I see that Viet cuisine is very flavorful and tasty, so how can I make it while there are not many Viet ingredients in the supermarket here in the UK?" and so on.

Therefore, with this book, I hope to bring Vietnamese cuisine closer to you. You will learn that Vietnamese foods are quick and easy to make, and easy to eat. You can find the ingredients in any Asian grocery store, and there are sources of alternative ingredients that you can easily access in Western supermarkets. People always say that when you know the cultural connotation behind a food, start to learn how to make some dishes, and use some unfamiliar tools and equipment for those dishes, you will discover the patterns and feel self-confident; thus, it will inspire you to go further into this cuisine.

A common Viet meal includes 3 major elements, such as a soup, a protein, or a stir-fry, that maybe different from your country's meals. The idea of having a Viet meal can be a good option for you when you would like to change your ordinary meals or enrich your weekends by adding a new food. Besides the change of palate, Vietnamese foods are really worth a try because they are healthy, delicious, and well-balanced. They are suitable for all age groups, particularly the elderly and children who need the nutrition, balance, and tenderness in their portions. Many dishes introduced in this book are super simple, often quick – just about 10 to 15 minutes to cook - and thus are suitable for working families. In addition, I have done some research to bring you wine pairings for authentic Vietnamese dishes, since wine is often served with meals in Western culture. Although drinking wine is not a part of Viet food culture, by interesting coincidence, the natural spiciness and saltiness in our food lets them match perfectly with wine.

What Makes Viet Cuisine Different?

In my own experience, Viet food is lighter, less spicy, and more flavorful than Thai food, though in the southern region of Vietnam, the cuisine shares some similarities with Thai and Cambodian food. People in the north and middle of Vietnam use more flavors, and these foods taste somehow sharper, less sweet, saltier, richer and more diverse. Northern Vietnamese cuisine is affected by Chinese food at some points, but it is less fatty, less sour, less spicy, and less bitter.

Unlike Chinese, Thai, or Japanese people who use soy sauce or oyster sauce as their main salty seasonings for cooking, Vietnamese use fish sauce, fermented soybeans, and seasoning powder.
Vietnamese cuisine represents five fundamental tastes (**ngũ vị**) in our meal. They are: sourness (wood), spiciness (metal), saltiness (water), sweetness (earth), and bitterness (fire). The five tastes are based on the philosophy that food, like human life, has five states, and can reflect emotional ups and downs. The harmonious combinations of elements lead to the success of a Viet dish. This differs from Thai food, where most dishes are a pattern of three tastes such as sweetness, saltiness, and sourness, with the last often the star of the dish. Viet cuisine also appreciates mouthfeel, unlike Japanese food, which highlights presentation, or Chinese and Western food, which cares more about the richness and fattiness. The fine taste of Viet food is achieved not only by the balance of

five tastes, but by combining the tastes with nutrition, fragrance, and color.

One of the crucial principles in creating a Viet meal is the concept of Yin and Yang. This is the philosophy of two opposite forces, for example female-male, black-white, negative-positive etc., forming a whole, attracting and complimenting each other. In cuisine, two opposite properties of ingredients are "hot" and "cool," which represent the contrasts in temperature and spiciness of the food, as well as the environment, and how they are combined with each other in a dish. This makes the food more balanced, and thus good for the health. For instance:

Salads with a lot of fresh vegetables are considered "cool," so they're most suitable for summer.

Sweet soups made of mung bean, black bean, and seaweed are meant to be refreshing, and are eaten in summer.

Seafoods and duck meat are considered "cool," and are typically balanced with "warm" ginger.

Meaningful And Essential Elements

Rice and salt are important elements in Viet cultural cuisine.

Vietnam is an agricultural country, and rice is grown in most fields, so rice plays a very important role in Viet culture. It is also seen as 'a gift from God'.

Rice and salt always go together to make a complete set for offering to the King of the Land, praying for a good harvest, or giving to the dead.

Bánh trưng, or Trưng cake, is the traditional Vietnamese glutinous rice cake. It's a square wrapped in green Dong leaves and filled with mung beans, pork, rice, and herbs. The glutinous rice for making the cake, 'Nếp cái hoa vàng', is aromatic and has big, round grains that differentiate it from Thai glutinous rice and its long, small grains. Banh Trưng symbolizes the earth, according to Viet's traditions.

Bánh dầy, or Dầy Cake, on the other hand, is associated with the sky. Bánh Trưng and bánh Dầy are often presented at the family ancestral altar during the Lunar New Year as an offering to the King of the Land and to the ancestors.

There are 3 types of rice in Vietnam: sticky rice, broken rice, and ordinary rice. Broken rice, or **gạo tấm**, is bits of whole grains broken during the milling process; it only has one name. Sticky rice can be named differently based on its shape, color and nutritional value. The two most popular are white and black sticky rice. Black rice is whole-grain produce, with its bran layer protein intact, so it is high in iron and crude fiber, and generally more nutritious than white rice. The most famous Vietnamese sticky rice brands are Nếp Cái Hoa Vàng white rice, and Nếp Cẩm or Nếp Than black sticky rice. Black rice is nuttier, chewier, and more nutritious than white rice, but black rice is not as popular. This may be because black rice isn't as sticky as white sticky rice, so most people will prefer the taste of white rice.

There are three varieties of ordinary rice: white, brown, and red. Like sticky rice, red and brown ordinary rice are more nutritious than white rice as they are known to be rich in iron, fiber and zinc. Vietnamese people have many types, but they often eat Gạo Tám, Gạo Nàng Thơm, Gạo Huyết Rồng, and Gạo Lứt due to their higher quality, aroma, and umami flavor.

In addition, there are many kinds of rice which are imported to Vietnam, such as Taiwan rice and Thai jasmine rice.

It's really unfortunate that, although Vietnamese rice is diverse and equal in quality to the rice of bigger exporters like Thailand, Taiwan, or Cambodia, we haven't exported much to the foreign markets, particularly European countries. This is due to the preference of the Vietnamese people and our marketing strategy to build our image and pass regulations. But if you make a trip to Vietnam, it's worth trying our rice.

'Tám' Rice

I really want to give ordinary rice, particularly 'Tám' rice, its own place in the book, as it deserves a spot. Ordinary rice is an integral dish in our daily meals and a basic necessity; 'Tám' rice is considered the best kind of ordinary rice in Vietnam, especially for northern people.

Tám rice has small, round, white grains. It is not to be confused with broken rice, or **gạo tấm**, like people in the south like to eat. There are 3 kinds of Tám rice, named after the provinces that produce the rice: Tám Xoan Hải hậu, Tám Điện biên, and Tám Hà Bắc. They are all aromatic, sticky, and tender when cooked. Tám Xoan Hải hậu has a longer, thinner shape than the other kinds. Once, Tám rice was often used for special occasions or for treating honoured guests. Nowadays, it's popular in daily Viet meals. I still believe it is the most delicious rice in Vietnam.

For the best result, Tám rice should be cooked by clay pot or cast-iron saucepan over a haybox cooker. However, many people often use an electric rice cooker for convenience and efficiency. Cooked tám rice is not served with soups but dry dishes like Vietnamese ham with some drops of fish sauce and ground pepper sprinkled on top.

Regional variations

As you may know, cuisine, like culture, is influenced by geography and climate conditions. While overall hot, humid, and experiencing monsoons, Vietnam has diverse geographic areas, three different cultures, and fifty-four ethnicities. Thus, Vietnamese culinary tradition differs from region to region, from North to Middle to South, creating the differences in Vietnamese regional cuisine.

The North

The North sticks out in my memory and has a special place in my heart, as this is where I was born and raised, and my mother is still living there. Hanoi, my home town, is located in the centre of the north considered the representative of northern cuisine, the cradle of internationally popular dishes like Phở; Spring Roll – **Nem Rán**; Steamed Rice Cake – **Bánh Cuốn**; Rice Noodle with Grilled Fish – **Chả cá Lã Vọng**; Green Papaya Salad - **Nộm đu đủ**; Noodles with Grilled Pork - **Bún Chả**; 'Thang' Noodles; 'Mọc' Noodles; Stir Fry Glass Noodles with Crab Meat – **Miến Xào Cua bể**, etc.

Climate

The climate here is the coldest to compare with the other parts of Vietnam so it's not a great place to plant herbs and spices. Thus, northern cuisine is not rooted in bold tastes or a variety of fresh herbs.

Light And Subtle

The main seasonings are light fish sauce and shrimp paste, followed by the sourness of vinegar and lime; sweetness is a rarity in our dishes. Food here is simpler than in other regions but it has its own delicate nature, eye-catching presentation, and complex, sophisticated cooking process.

Special Ingredients

Sấu (dracontomelon) and Mẻ (fermented cooked rice) are the main sources of sourness in the north of Vietnam. Popular in soups, these ingredients make food taste fragrant and slightly sour, and give food a different mouthfeel than other sour sources like lime and vinegar. Apart from soup, Sấu is also used for making soft drink by soaking in salt or sugar for about 1-2 weeks. It is one of four fundamental ingredients for a very delicious dipping sauce, the others being fish sauce, chili pepper, and garlic. Sấu in Ô mai Sấu (Sugared fry Sấu) is a Hanoi specialty that any traveler who visits Hanoi would hear about, and when they leave, these travelers always buy it as a present for their friends and loved ones back in their hometown.

Fermented Soybeans (Tương Bần)

While the South is known for fermented anchovy, the North is known for fermented soybeans. It comes in a liquid form, and the taste is salty and fragrant. It really boost the flavors of different sauces, soups, and dips.

The Central Region

Standing in the heart of Central Vietnam is the city of Hue, the former imperial capital during the Nguyen Dynasty emperors between 1802–1945, today notable for its imperial cuisine. The culinary tradition features most complex, colorful, flavorful and sophisticated food.

The other aspect that defines this land is the much more severe weather than the other regions of Vietnam. The people here are known for being thrifty and outspoken, and this reflected in their food.

Spicy And Bold

Unlike the mild flavors of northern cuisine, central food has bold and spicy flavors. A large number of chilies are used in most dishes, and salty flavors are sharp and strong. The food is often divided in small portions. Due to regular crop failures during the year, the people here, particularly farmers and fishermen, got into the habit of cooking food in bulk, adding a lot of salt, and eating a little at a time so the food could last as long as possible.

Imperial Cuisine

Apart from common people in the suburbs, central cuisine is inspired by the great affluence of the imperial palace, particularly in Hue city. The Emperors would normally require food that was much more artistic, more elegant, and more aesthetically pleasing. The ingredients are more diverse and flavors are well balanced and delicate.

Iconic Dishes

- Spring Rolls with Prawn - **Nem rán nhân Tôm**
- Khoai Crape - **Bánh Khoái** (a small version of Bánh Xèo)
- Fish Grilled in Banana Leaves - **Cá nướng lá chuối**
- Husband and Wife Cake - **Bánh Phu Thê**
- Tam Ky Chicken Rice - **Cơm gà Tam Kỳ**
- Quang Noodles – **Mỳ Quảng**
- Hue Beef Noodles – **Bún bò Huế** (recipe in Part 2)
- Shrimp Wrapped around Sugar Cane - **Chạo Tôm**

The South

I have spent more than ten years living in the south of Vietnam and the land has left a deep impression on my mind. The dynamic, the economic growth, the fashion of the country - all of that, and more, can be found here. People who have come to Vietnam often know about the south of Vietnam as it has its famous city – Ho Chi Minh City or Saigon.

I would like to combine the south with the south east and the west due to their similarity in culture, weather, and the hospitality of the people. With that definition, Mekong Delta's fabulously fertile soil, together with the region's warm weather, create perfect conditions for planting a wide variety of fruits and vegetables, fishing, and raising livestock. As a result, the flavors of ingredients are much more overwhelming. The climate here is naturally less severe than the other parts of Vietnam. You rarely see storms and floods so southern people, unlike northern and central people, don't tend to "an cư lạc nghiệp" (meaning "to settle down") by building a firm foundation where they live. Instead, they spend money more hedonistically. That's the main reason why southerners are characterized as more free-spirited, generous, wild, and enthusiastic. Their food also reflects such traits.

Sweet And Rich

The Southwest and South Central of Vietnam share a border with Cambodia and are close to Thailand, so they share many culinary similarities. However, we add our own flavor to particular food and make it our own way. For example, Thai people add coconut milk to their soups, but Viet cuisine prefers clear broth. Therefore, we often separate coconut milk into two parts; one is diluted and used for soups, while the other is mostly used to garnish our dishes.

Southern cuisine is sweeter, balancing the saltiness. Enriching soups, crepes, and cakes is a feature of the cuisine here, like in the iconic Bánh Xèo - Xeo Crepe, Chuối Nướng - Grilled Banana, Chè Bắp - Corn Sweet Soup, or Thịt kho Trứng - Caramelized Pork with Eggs.

Seafood And Fermented Anchovy Sauces

The South is known for a wide variety of seafood and fermented anchovy sauces. No other parts of Vietnam have such culinary richness. There are numerous kinds of brackish water and saltwater seafood like shrimp, shellfish, crab, and snail, and the vast quantities of them can be used for making fermented paste such as Cá Sặc - Gourami, Cá Linh - Mud Carp, Bò hóc - Prahok, Ba Khía - Sesarma Mederi etc.

I could not forget the time when I travelled to An Giang province during the flooding season, which roughly starts between August and November every year. I saw a lot of mud carps floating on the water and even stuck on the banks of the river. Young mud carp tastes sweet, fatty, and spineless, and it is the main ingredient for many specialties in the Southwest, including Mắm Nêm - Fermented Anchovy Paste, and Lẩu Mắm - Seafood Hotpot using fermented mud carp and braised mud carp.

Unique Ingredients

The South is where special ingredients, like Hoa Điên Điển - Common Sesban,
Lá Vông - Sunshine Tree, and even field mice, bat, cobra, and mud clam are used in cooking.

Due to the abundance of fresh herbs and natural products, together with the liberal lifestyle, southern cuisine is notable for its wildness and generosity. This is reflected in daily meals through dishes made by wild plants, animals, and insects.

Iconic Dishes:

- **Hủ Tiếu -** Rice Noodle with Pork and Seafood
- **Canh chua Cá Lóc -** Sour Soup (recipe in Part 2)
- **Bánh Canh Trảng Bàng –** Trang Bang Thick Noodle Soup
  - Cá kèo kho tộ - **Braised Elongatus**
- **Bún Mắm -** Fermented Fish Noodle Soup
- **Thịt kho Trứng -** Cameralized Pork with Eggs (recipe in Part 2)

Common Features

Despite the differences, regions in Vietnam share common features when it comes to cuisine. There's no starter course in a traditional Viet meal; it starts with soup, mostly vegetable soup, then the main courses are served with cooked rice. Rice plays a crucial role in typical family meals. Unlike Western people, Vietnamese do not eat bread or noodles in our main courses, though you can regularly see the appearance of noodle and bread in our quick meals like breakfast or lunch, in the street restaurants or at roadside stands.

The main flavors are fermented fish, fish sauce, fermented soybeans, soy sauce, fermented krill-shrimp paste, and seasoning-cooking powder. This sounds to foreigners like Viet foods are bold and flavorful, but actually using fresh herbs, fruits, vegetables, and especially fat, is a rarity in our food and the perfect balance between fresh herbs and meats in meal portions make Viet food one of the healthiest cuisines in the world.

Inside Xom Chieu Market in Ho Chi Minh City: Different types of fermented fish and fish sauces.

Influence of Culture on What People Eat

Culinary culture originated in ordinary life. It began with simple family meals, environment, climate, history, and belief of a region. No one denies that culture has a big influence on any cuisine, where through the dining etiquette, people can demystify the human value and discover a nation's morals, manners, and customs.

I was born and raised in Vietnam, where the culture features diverse, delicious, fatless, flavor-rich, and healthy gastronomies. Although I have lived in London for almost 6 years I always try to get a bite of my native food whenever I can, and that is usually cooked at my rental flat in London.

Right after I moved here, I quickly discovered that there were Vietnamese restaurants in London, mostly in the south, east, and north, with some in the southwest and central city. I've visited some of them, but sadly, I haven't found the authentic ones. I guess this is because there are no exact flavors and ingredients like there are back in Vietnam, and the restaurants owners all change the tastes in order to meet the palate of people living here in London.

Culinary culture differs from country to country, not only in term of what we eat but also the amount we eat and how we eat. In Western culture, for example, people tend to have their own individual plate of food, and the serving size of protein is essentially bigger. In

Vietnam, we eat out of a shared bowl and the amount we eat once at a time is just about a regular size compared with a Western portion. In a Vietnamese meal, there is a tray in the middle of dining table, we eat with chopsticks, and cooked rice is an essential part of a meal. In the north of Vietnam people used to invite each other before starting the meal. This invitation often comes from the youngest persons present at the meal first, then someone older. However, this is not the case of the other parts of the country.

In Vietnam, every dish is eaten with cooked rice, which is communal and to be shared in the middle of the table. It is our tradition that members of a family often wait until the last member joins and sits around the rice tray to get the meal started. It is common for a person who sits right next to the rice cooker to serve rice for other people, often serving the elderly and guests first as a display of respect and a gesture of kindness. At a large table, where you can reach a dish but the other people can not, it is a good etiquette to ask others if they would like to be served, and if they would, you pick up food for them as an action of care.

Drinking Culture - Văn hoá Nhậu

I debated whether or not to include this topic in the book, but finally I decided to add it here as it vividly reflects a cultural aspect in Viet cuisine.

Definition of "Nhậu" in Vietnam

There's a saying amongst drinkers in Vietnam that "a man without booze is like a placid flag on a windless day". A majority of men in Vietnam can drink, or **nhậu**, while the number of women who drink, luckily, stays below 2%. Alcohol, particularly beer, is very cheap, so bars or brasseries are the common destinations for drinkers all over Vietnam.

You can hear some sayings in Vietnam like "drunk first, home later" or "proper drinking means turning drunk". I believe these are only said between a minority of drinkers, and not considered an aspect of the drinking culture of our country at all. Nowadays, it's not rare to see people meet each other and discuss a business transaction around a drinking table.

Having said all that about drinking, I can't help but look to the south of Vietnam, including the west and east regions I discussed earlier, where drinking culture has become deeply ingrained into daily life. Happiness is a reason for drinking, sadness is also a reason for drinking; meetings: drinking; special occasions: drinking; no special dates, no reason to be happy or sad: drinking. 'Drinking' here means genuine, hard drinking - not just some glasses of beer, but homemade brandy as well. Wine distilled at home by the traditional way has a quite high alcohol content, around 30-40%. It's usually made from whole grain like rice, corn, cassava, or oats, or made from different seeds like **Musa balbisiana.** One type of unique Vietnamese wine is called "Rượu Cần", made with rice and a mixture of various herbs, with a strength ranging from 15 to 25% alcohol by volume.

You don't need much for serving drinks; some guavas, some ambarellas, a plate of roasted peanut, or some grilled dried fishes are enough for an overnight drinking party. It may be because of drinking habits, but I don't often see the drinkers get drunk; they only get tipsy, enough for cheering up to have open-hearted chats. Drinking is a means for interaction and relaxation. However, inevitably, there are people who drink so much that they forget the way back home. It's nothing glamorous, but this is one side of our drinking lives.

The drinking life in Vietnam must have made an impression on travelers, because booze is sold almost everywhere, on every street. This is very different from other countries; for example, in England, where I am living, the sale and consumption of alcohol is restricted by license, by the time of day, by the age at which people are allowed to purchase alcohol, etc. In order to serve so many drinkers, Vietnamese cuisine becomes more diverse; there are thousands of dishes made for serving with beverages. These dishes, according to recent trends, are to be simple, flexible, low in fat, and cheap.

What 'Real' Drinkers Serve with Booze

Vietnamese people don't pick specific foods to pair with booze because if there's a chance to talk and share with friends or relatives, we often bring almost all the food we have on hand to treat our guests. However, 'real' drinkers have a clear distinction:

For drinking beer:
Drinkers usually like to serve beer with dried dishes such as beef jerky, buffalo jerky, grilled dried squid, roasted peanuts, stir-fried snails, or dishes made from insects like deep-fried cricket, scorpion, or cicada.

For wine:
Food is often richer, including both dried dishes and soups. The favourite dishes are often named, and include grilled, boiled, steamed, and stir-fried dishes made from pork meat, dog meat, or fish. Other popular foods are soups like sour shrimp soup and hotpots; dishes made from chicken feet, such as chicken feet mixed with spices, or grilled with salt and hot chili; and salads like fig salad, lotus delight salad, and chicken salad with Vietnamese coriander.

National Drinks

Drinking trends contribute to the creation of wine brands, for both Vietnamese people and foreigners. The top five are Gò Đen in the south region, Bàu Đá in the middle of Vietnam, Đà Lạt in the highland, and Làng Vân and Mẫu Sơn in northern Vietnam.

Due to the prevalence of rich street food and the tropical climate, light beer is a popular beverage. Draft Beer (Bia Hơi) dominates the street restaurants. Other Vietnamese beer brands still find their niche, typically in a regional market; Bia Sài Gòn is a product of Saigon, Bia Hà Nội is made in Hanoi, and Bia Huda comes from Huế, the central region of Vietnam.

Outside a beer stall in Hanoi

On Beverage Pairing

Beer Pairing

It doesn't matter if you're rich, poor, or middle-class; when you come to Vietnam you'll find large crowds of people sitting in beer halls. These halls usually have only a tiny indoor space, mainly for storage and food preparation. The seating is almost entirely outside, only equipped with small plastic stools that people use for both seating and holding food and beers (image attached).

Besides national-branded beer, Vietnam is also notable for its brandless beer - fresh beer or **'bia hơi'**. 'Bia hoi', unlike Western beer or canned/branded beer, is made with 50% rice. It is also unpreserved, brewed daily, and has a low alcohol volume (1.5 to 2%). The climate of Vietnam, where hot weather is common, makes light beer with refreshing flavors favourable.

However, when winter comes, darker beer is welcomed. Tiger, Heineken, and Guinness are our most popular imports, bringing diverse flavors to our beverage selection.

Like wine, beer should also be matched with food. The bitter taste of beer needs to be combined with low-acidity food, and helps to withstand the saltiness and spiciness of many dishes. Once again, there's a good news! There are a lot of spicy and salty dishes in Viet cuisine.

Wine Pairing

When you drink wine, what foods do you think match well with it? In order to answer this question, I think we should start with what we know about the main tastes of wine.

When you drink white wine, the tastes left on your tongue should be sourness and sweetness. Foods served with white wines should not be sweeter than wine, or the wine will taste sour. This makes food from northern and central Vietnam work particularly well with wine, since many dishes aren't very sweet. Southern foods match well with sweeter wines like Chenin Blanc, Pinot Gris, or Moscato.

Red wine is another story. The body of red wine has tannin, giving it a dry or astringent character. Any time you drink Merlot, Malbec, Pinot Noir, or Cabernet Sauvignon, you can feel that drying sensation in your mouth. Going to a party and drinking red wine? Remember to select hearty dishes with ingredients like beef, lamb, or other red meat; otherwise, you should pick out a white wine instead. Vietnamese cuisine doesn't have a wide variety of foods that pair well with red wine as we don't often drink wine with our meals like Westerners do. It's best to choose choose a high-acid, low-tannin bottle of red wine when you are in Vietnam.

Vietnamese Wine

Traditional Vietnamese wine is made from rice, cassava or corn. French colonists turned their attention to fruit wine production in the late 19th century, and as a result, wine made from a variety of grapes is popular nowadays.

Distilled wine (Rượu đế) is made of either glutinous or non-glutinous rice. Its strength varies, but is typically 40 percent alcohol by volume. It is usually clear or a bit cloudy in appearance. Rượu đế is popular with the majority of commoners. It's sold at a low price and works well with simple foods like grilled cá lóc, or just a bite of green mango.

Soaked wine (Rượu thuốc) is made by soaking herbs or animals in high-quality distilled white wine. Many believe that this kind of liquor helps boost the health and virility of men.

Undistilled wine (Rượu bổ) is formed by the natural fermenting process of fruits, trees, flowers, and glutinous rice. These wines are popular in ethnic minority areas.

People go to beer halls not just for the drinking experience, but the great food; most bia hoi offer fresh and skillfully prepared dishes for very little cost. You can reliably find many foods like banana flower salad, barbecued chicken and fried rice, deep-fried pork ribs, and lemongrass chicken. The best suited foods for pairing with wine or beer are grilled, dried foods like grilled squid, grilled dried fish such as dried stingray, yellowstripe scad, gourami, deer jerky; beef jerky; and spicy dried squid/shrimp **(recipe in Part 2)**.

Pickles: most popular fruits like green mango and ambarella are finely chopped and mix with minced garlic, chilli pepper, salting agents, acids and/or with different types of dried fish.

Other dried dishes include roasted peanuts **(recipe in Part 2)** cured in flavoring powder and roasted rice wafers.

I have recipes that work well with beer and wine in Part 2, Chapter: Foods Match with Alcohol.

How to construct a Viet Meal

A typical Vietnamese meal for the average family has at least five dishes and often includes:
Individual bowls of rice
One or two dishes with protein
One stir-fry dish
Raw, pickled, steamed, or fresh vegetables
One broth or soup
Dipping sauces and condiments (to which garlic, pepper, chili, ginger, or lime juice are sometimes added according to taste)
Desserts are often served with fresh fruits or puddings.
Vietnamese often eat fresh foods, like live fish or 'hot' meat that's just come from the abattoir. It's common for housewives to go to the market or supermarket early in the morning in order to pick the freshest ingredients. The balance of the main ingredient is also important. You should have an assortment of fish, meat, shellfish, poultry, vegetables, eggs, etc. Having repeats is fine when you have several dishes, but when there are only three or four, the meal is better balanced if all the dishes feature a different main ingredient.
A well-balanced meal is a meal with at least four elements: protein, chat bot, fiber, and water or liquid. As the main ingredient, the proportion of protein is not as huge as in Western cooking, but it is only a part of

the meal; other ingredients come into play, particularly vegetables.

One-Dish Meal

Besides family-style dining, where foods are shared among members, Vietnam has another type of meal called a one-dish meal. A one-dish meal is a complete meal on its own, not meant to be shared with anyone. These are often breakfasts or quick lunches, but not served in family dinners.

One of the most popular one-dish meals that you should try is Banh Mi, the Vietnamese Sandwich. Some others are noodle soups, broken rice with grilled pork (**cơm tấm**), sticky rice (**xôi**), steamed buns (**bánh bao**), and rolled cakes (**các món cuốn**).

Pictures taken in Mo Market, Hanoi — Left to right: Hot Chili sauce, Hoisin sauce, fermented soybean sauce, shrimp paste, liquid caramel, soy sauce, lemon sauce, salad dressing.

Condiments and Seasonings

Unlike Western eateries, where you can find ketchup, mustard, gravy, salt, and pepper, we have many options depending on what you are eating. Here are the most common and important ones:

Mắm Tôm: Mắm means paste and tôm is shrimp. This condiment is made from fermented shrimp and often added to Bún Riêu Cua (bún means noodles, while riêu cua is little crab soup).

Nước Mắm (Fish Sauce) can be used as it is, or mixed with lemon juice, garlic, vinegar, sugar, and chili to make a light dipping sauce.

Tương Bần is made from fermented soybeans and other ingredients such as glutinous rice, salt, and fermenting agent. It's considered the most umami condiment in Vietnam and often used for braised, steamed recipes, soups, and sauces for boiled dishes.

Soy sauce is mostly is used in marinades and sauces.

Hoisin sauce is used in Southern Vietnam to mix with **phở** (noodles) while serving.

Hot chili sauce is used in Phở or straight-up fish sauce.

Salting agents include table salt (muối), seasoning powder (bột canh), and broth mix (hạt nêm)

Seasoning Powder or Bột Canh

This is one of the main salty agents in Vietnamese cuisine. The ingredients of seasoning powder include salt, sugar, flavor enhancer, and spices such as garlic powder, ground pepper, chili powder, and dried green onion. Seasoning powder's texture is smoother than broth mix, so it can be used for making dips for foods, particularly grilled seafoods and fresh fruits. It is also often used for marinating and cooking.

There are two types of seasoning powder: vegetarian and non-vegetarian. Non-vegetarian seasoning powder has meat flavor in the ingredients; the most popular flavors are chicken and shrimp. Vegetarian flavors are available, too, like shiitake mushroom.

Broth Mix or Hạt Nêm

The major ingredient, about 98%, of seasoning powder is MSG - monosodium glutamate - or other meat-flavor enhancers. The other element is powder which comes from animal meat (mostly chicken or shrimp). It creates a light sweetness to stimulate your taste buds. Although there's a lot of MSG in broth mix, it is proven to be non-toxic if used in reasonable amounts.

Like seasoning powder, broth mix also comes with two types, vegetarian and non-vegetarian.

Acids include lime (chanh), sliced garlics and spur chillies pickled in white vinegar (dấm tỏi), and kumquat (trái tắc/quất).

Sweetness comes from granulated sugar (đường cát), rock sugar (đường phèn), cane sugar (đường phèn), brown sugar (đường vàng), and palm sugar (đường thốt nốt).

Spiciness can be added with chili peppers (ớt), fried chili flakes in oil (sa tế), black/white pepper (tiêu đen/trắng), chili sauce (tương ớt), or chili powder (ớt bột).

Condiments for noodles in the south of Vietnam.

Condiments for noodles soup 'Pho': Left to right: Pickled Garlic and Hot chili, Hot chili sauce, Broth mix, Ground Pepper

Understanding Key Ingredients for Vietnamese Cooking
Vietnamese cuisine wins diners' hearts not with individual foods like caviar, shark fin, or abalone, but by balancing the combination of ingredients to ensure the food is not too spicy, not too fatty, and not too sweet. The richness in spices, fresh herbs, and vegetables is also a major plus for Viet cuisine.

Herbs & Vegetables

Herbs

Below: left to right: Chinese celery, Chives, Sawtooth
Above: left to right: Vietnamese Green Onions, Knotgrass

TURMERIC - Nghệ

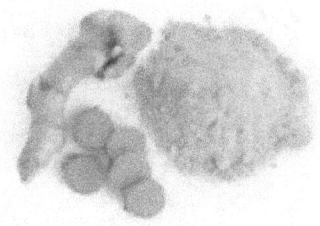

In Vietnam, turmeric is considered as an elixir, since can be used to treat stomach ulcers, lower cholesterol, and make your skin beautiful. It's also used as a spice in many dishes. It has a beautiful color, mild aroma, and a very warm and musky flavor with little hints of bitter and sour. Using turmeric in cooking not only adds color and enhances the flavor of food, but also brings fantastic health benefits.

There are delicious dishes that are suitable for adding turmeric. They are:

Noodles stir-fried with pork meat, pork heart, kidney.
Fish (brackish water fish) Soup
Braised Fish (brackish and saltwater fish) with Turmeric
Grilled Salmon with Turmeric
Chicken Curry

How to use

Turmeric can be used fresh or in the form of starch. In everyday life, people prefer using turmeric starch for convenience and to reduce the side effects. Fresh turmeric has an amount of oil that is not good for the human body.

LEMONGRASS - Sả

Lemongrass is commonly used in Vietnamese cooking as it adds a lemony aroma to the dish.

There are common dishes that use lemongrass:

Chicken Curry - Cà ri gà

Beef Stew - Bò kho

Lime & Lemongrass Drink - Nước chanh sả

Spicy Lemongrass Chicken - Gà xào sả ớt

How to use

On the thick, white part of the root, cut off the root end. Then discard one or two of the outer leaves, which are normally dry and dirty. When you reach the moist and tender part, you've found the part of the plant used in cooking.

You can use the stalk for cooking - mostly for making stock or tea. You can smash the lemongrass for a flavor infusion, as smashing helps release the fragrance. In this case make sure you remove the stalk from the dish before serving. If you would like to eat lemongrass you can finely slice it or transform it into a paste.

Lemongrass can be stored in the freezer for weeks, but remember to dry it first. Wrap every single one, two, or other amount of lemongrass in cling film, depending on how much you use at once. Package it in a thick waterproof bag suitable for the freezer. Be sure to squeeze out as much air as possible when packaging.

GALANGAL - Riềng

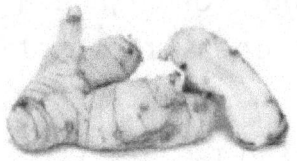

Galangal is a fragrant root that looks like ginger. However, galangal has a cooler and more treelike flavor.

Galangal can be imported fresh, but in Western countries, you'll find most galangal is frozen or dried. The fresh galangal is more tender and easier to process for your cooking. Galangal is firm, so whether you have fresh, dried or frozen galangal on hand, the best way to use it is to soak it in water overnight before slicing it.

There are popular dishes that use galangal:

Mocked Dog - Giả cầy **(recipe in Part 2)**

Braised Mackerel with Galangal - Cá thu kho riềng

Grilled Catfish with Fermented Rice & Galangal

Beef Stew - Bò kho

How to use

You don't have to peel galangal before using, but if there are blemishes on the skin you should cut them off. The young, yellow-and-white part is edible and is the most tender. Discard the pinkish part.

Like lemongrass, galangal can be processed into different forms. Thin slices of galangal can be used to infuse hot liquids, but be sure you remove the slices before serving. You also can julienne or grind galangal down into a paste for easier marinating or stir-fries.

How to store

Galangal is stored in the freezer to retain its quality, like lemongrass.

GINGER - Gừng

Ginger, like garlic and shallots, have become essential items in Vietnamese cooking. Some assume that the use of these herbs were influenced by the Chinese, but in fact, the Vietnamese herbs are different. Vietnamese ginger is smaller and more fragrant, the trunk has more branches, and the skin has more blemishes.

How to use

Ginger doesn't need to be peeled before using. It can be cut into thin slices and infused in hot liquid or dried for candied fruits. It can also be finely shredded and added to sweet soups, stir-fries, bone soup, steamed dishes, or used in recipes for tea, cookies, and wine.

Picking a good-quality piece of ginger helps you get more flavor out of it, and it will last longer. For fresh ginger, look for pieces that are firm, heavy, succulent, light in color, and lively. Fresh ginger has a spicy, dark flavor and aroma.

How to store

You can store whole ginger in the freezer for up to six months in a plastic bag. Actually, ginger is easier to chop when it is frozen, as it seems less fibrous than fresh ginger.

Ginger can stay fresh for about 2 weeks in the fridge, but be sure to wrap it carefully in tissue paper, then fold in cling film.

You can also let it stay outside at room temperature, but be sure to keep it away from sunlight and moisture; sunlight will cause ginger to lose its flavor and moisture will make it moldy.

Foods are suitable for adding ginger:

Caramelized Chicken with Mushroom and Ginger **(recipe in Part 2)**

Candied Ginger

Tea with Ginger

Braised Duck with Ginger

CORIANDER – Ngò

In Vietnam, coriander stems and roots are rarely used for cooking, but coriander leaves are a popular garnish. You can keep coriander fresh for about a week if you store it in a zipper bag and place it in the fridge. Just be sure to wash and dry the leaves carefully before storing.

THAI BASIL - Húng quế

Thai Basil is also called sweet basil, as it has a sweet flavor. It's also very fragrant, refreshing, and acrid. There are various kinds of basil, with big or small leaves, round or oval leaves, purple or green stems, or the entire plant could be purple or green.
Thai basil in Vietnam has a lighter, cinnamon-like flavor. It's often used in blood soup (tiết canh), grilled pork with vermicelli, Hue beef noodles, and southern-style Phở. The seeds of the basil plant, called hạt é, are ingredients for refreshing drinks, particularly glass jelly.

SAWTOOTH CORIANDER - ngò gai or mùi tàu

Sawtooth coriander has small, long leaves with thorny edges. It has a comfortable, refreshing flavor and it pairs well with Phở **(recipe in Part 2)** and Sour Soup **(recipe in Part 2)**.

ENYDRA FLUCTUANS - rau ngổ or rau ôm

Enydra fluctuans, or buffalo spinach, is a plant that you can find in large quantities on the edges of rice fields or ponds, as it is easy to grow like a weed. It has a piquant, slightly sour, refreshing, and very fragrant flavor. Like sawtooth coriander, enydra fluctuans do not withstand cooking well at all, so it is often used as a garnish for soups or stir-fries.

SPEARMINT - bạc hà or húng lủi/húng láng

Spearmint carries a lot of names, from bạc hà and húng láng, like people in the north of Vietnam often call it; to húng lủi, the name southern Vietnamese use. This herbal plant grows on the surface of the ground. The leaves are small and long, with thorny edges and a lot of fragrance. You can eat the whole plant, including stems and leaves. Spearmint is often used as a garnish or side-table vegetable for famous dishes like Phở or Grilled Chicken.

ELSHOLTZIA CILIATA - kinh giới

Kinh giới is a flowery plant with a straight, square-shaped stem that is very popular in every part of Vietnam. We don't use the stem of kinh giới, but its leaves are used as a fragrant herb and are essential part of a well-known dish: Green Papaya Salad **(recipe in Part 2).**

HEARTLEAF - diếp cá or giấp cá

This herbal plant is only available in Asian countries. Diếp cá can be found growing in the wild in humid place. Like its name suggests, the leaves have a heart shape, and when you rub them the leaves release a foul smell. Despite this, heartleaf has a refreshing, sour, and spicy flavor which makes it pair well with salads or side-table vegetables. Heartleaf can withstand cooking so it is not only used in cold food such as salads and dips but also hot food like Grilled Beef Wrapped in Betel Leaves **(recipe in Part 2)**.

PERILLA - tía tô

The perilla plant shares some similarities with heartleaf, as it is only popular in Asian countries and it withstands cooking. You can find perilla in cooked soup, such as Eggplant and Perilla Soup, as well as raw and mixed vegetables for salads or noodles. However, there are differences: you can use the whole perilla plant, including stems, leaves, and even seeds, and it is a common herb throughout Vietnam while heartleaf is most popular in the south of Vietnam.

VIETNAMESE CORIANDER - **rau răm**

Vietnamese coriander leaves and young stems are used widely in Southeast Asian cuisine. It has a pungent, spicy, and fragrant flavor. It is primary eaten raw or cut into fine pieces which are added to soups such as 'Thang' noodle soup **(recipe in Part 2),** congees such as snail congee, or salads like chicken salad **(recipe in Part 2).**

Vegetables

Left to right: Green Amaranth, Red Amaranth, Water spinach

CHINESE CELERY - **cần tây**

Chinese celery is widely available in the winter time in Vietnam, especially before Lunar New Year (Tết). It can withstand cooking and often be used in stir-fries, like beef stir-fry, and in noodles soup such as Nam Vang Noodles Soup (Hủ tiếu Nam Vang).

WATER DROPWORT - cần nước

Water dropwort is an aquatic plant with small, long, round, stems and many knuckles. In Vietnam, water dropwort has become popular in daily family meals and it can be cooked into various dishes including stir-fries like Stir-Fry Beef with Water Dropwort, salads such as Water Dropwort Salad, or noodle soups like Noodle Soup with Anabas.

INDIAN TARO - dọc mùng or bạc hà

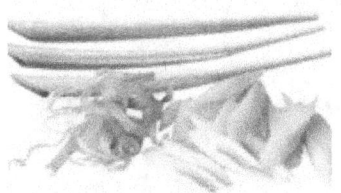

Indian Taro is known as Dọc Mùng in northern Vietnam or Bạc Hà in southern Vietnam. We use the the leaf stalk of the Indian Taro plant in dishes like Sour Soup (canh chua) **(recipe in Part 2)** and Noodle with Indian Taro and Pork Hock (bún móng giò dọc mùng)

KNOTGRASS - **rau đắng**

Rau đắng comes from a flowery evergreen herb. The leaves and younger parts of knotgrass are edible and often used for cooking soups or hot pots, or simply eaten raw. When you first taste knotgrass, you may think it has a bitter flavor, but if you eat it more frequently you can taste a sweetness which many people say is unforgettable.

CENTELLA - **Rau má**

Centella is a kind of creeping vegetable with a long, smooth, thin, and white-green stem and white root. Rau má has refreshing, bitter, spicy flavor. The whole centella plant is edible including root, stem, and leaf, and it's mostly used for fresh and nutritious drinks, salads, or steamed dishes.

LOTUS STEM - **Ngó sen**

Lotus stem is the rhizome part of the lotus flower, just below the stump. In order to nip it off, the lotus planters have to stand up to the chest in the mud, bend over to find the lotus stem, and nip them off one at a time. A good-quality lotus stem is about 25 cm long, very white, smooth, and cool. It has a super refreshing, naturally sweet flavor and a nice crunch. It is considered a vegetable and often used in stir-fries, pickles, and internationally common salads like Lotus Stem Salad with Pork and Shrimp.

BANANA FLOWER - Hoa chuối or Bắp chuối

Banana flowers come from the stem of the banana tree. Most widely grown banana trees have red flowers, but home planted trees have violet flowers. I don't know the reason why that is, and no one really cares about it. We only care about the quality of the tree in general and the flower specifically. Banana flowers are very rich in vitamins A and C, minerals, fiber, and manganese; they are slightly bitter but very crunchy and refreshing, so they are often used as the main ingredient for salads, sour soups, or side-table vegetables for noodle soups like Mocked Dog (Thịt heo giả cầy) **(recipe in Part 2).**

WATER SPINACH - **rau muống**

Water spinach is one of the most popular and beloved vegetables in Vietnam. It can be grown both in the soil and in water. Its stems are thick, light green, and airy, while the triangular leaves have sharp ends and can be big and round or small and long. Normally, water spinach plants that grow naturally on, or are planted in the water have big, round leaves, and are purple in color. If cultivated on land, it is white with small, long leaves. In London, where I am living, I only can find white water spinach. In cooking, water spinach is often boiled or stir-fried with garlic and beef, though it also can be used for salads or soups.

CABBAGE/NAPA CABBAGE/CAULIFLOWER/BROCCOLI/PAK CHOY/BOK CHOY/MUSTARD GREEN/CHOY SUM/WHITE RADISH/RED BEET
bắp cải/cải thảo/hoa lơ or súp lơ/bông cải xanh/cải bẹ

trắng/cải thìa/cải bẹ xanh/cải ngọt/củ cải trắng/củ cải đỏ

I like to group these together as they are all of the Chinese cabbage family. They are actually from temperate climates. Nowadays you can see Chinese cabbages planted everywhere in the world, including tropical countries. In Vietnam, you can see them in the winter or spring in the north and central regions, or they can be found throughout the year in the south, brought in from the cool highlands of Dalat.

Chinese cabbages often have sweet, refreshing, and rich in vitamins and minerals. They are also easy to eat, easy to process and are frequently used for stir-fries, soups, or simply just for a boiled dish or side-table vegetables for hot pot.

What About Other Vegetables?

There are numerous kinds of exotic vegetables which are hard to find in many parts of the world. Here is a list of some:

SWEET LEAF - **rau ngót**
TELOSMA CORDATA - **hoa thiên lý**
WATERCRESS - **cải xoong**
GARLAND CHRYSANTHEMUM - **cải cúc or tần ô**
CHAYOTE - **Su su**
JUTE PLANT - rau đay
AMARANTH - **rau dền**
BITTER MELON - **khổ qua, mướp đắng**
KOHLRABI - **su hào**

JICAMA - **củ đậu**
LOOFAH/LUFFA/SPONGE GOURD - **mướp**

Khổ qua - Bitter Melon Mướp hương – Sponge Gourd

There are numerous exotic dishes made with these ingredients. Don't be overwhelmed; if you are living in a place where you cannot get this produce fresh, or at all, there is always an alternative. Cooking needs to be creative in this respect, and you can have a lot of fun making something new from the 'old' ingredients available in your area. The outcome, I'm pretty sure, should be very much similar to the authentic dishes. For example, when making spring rolls, I use onion instead of jicama, as onion works very well with the other ingredients in the filling. The taste, texture, and color are similar to jicama, which I rarely can find in London, and if I am lucky enough to see it in Asian grocery store it's often very expensive.

It's the same with spices. I love soy sauce and oyster sauce, as these can be used in place of cooking powder, the traditional Vietnamese spice, and impart the perfect result for the dish.

The recipes in this book are written using vegetables that are common and available in Vietnam. I see that is a challenge for many people who have never seen or even heard about these ingredients. In order to encourage you to try cooking Vietnamese food and not give up, I'll give you some ideas of ingredient substitutions in the chapter "Suggestions for Ingredient Substitutions".

Dried Spices

STAR ANISE - **hoa hồi**

From the name of star anise you can guess that, indeed, it has a star shape with a diameter of about 2.5cm-3cm. It has a warm, very strong flavor and it smells like licorice. Star anise is one component of five-spice powder, and is an essential part of Phở's broth, chicken curry, beef stew, and other steamed dishes as it adds nutrition and enhances the flavor of the dish.

How to use
Star Anise comes powdered or dried. T most popular kind you can find is whole dried seed. Be sure to dry-fry or grill it before cooking so it can impart the best flavor. Due to its strong smell, be careful not to add too much to your food, as it may impart an uncomfortable taste. As whole seeds, star anise cannot be eaten so make sure to remove it when serving. In powdered form, star anise can be used as part of a soup.

CINNAMON - **quế**

Cinnamon is the outside (vỏ) of the cinnamon tree. It has a spicy and fragrant flavor and, like star anise, it's one spice of five-spice powder. It's also used in making Phở's broth and various Vietnamese soups. Cinnamon isn't as strong as star anise, so you can be a little bit more liberal in using it.

How to use
Cinnamon comes in the same forms as star anise: dried or powdered. You may not find it in its whole form, however. A cinnamon bar should be grilled or dry-fried before cooking so it can impart the best flavor. In powdered form, cinnamon can be used as part of a dish.

CARDAMOM - **thảo quả**

Cardamom is the pod from a flowering plant belonging to the ginger family. It can be used as a medicine in Chinese herbs, or a spice in Chinese and Vietnamese cuisines. Cardamom has a smoky, spicy, warm, and slightly bitter flavor and aroma.

The pods are often used as an important ingredient in the broth for the Vietnamese specialty - noodle soup Phở.

How to use

Cardamom, like other dried spices, often comes dried or powdered. In whole seed pods, cardamom cannot be eaten, so make sure to avoid it when serving. Just be sure to dry-fry or grill it before cooking so it can give your food the best flavor. In powdered form, cardamom can be used as part of a soup.

ANNATTO SEEDS - hạt điều

Annatto seeds are meaty, dark reddish pods from annatto plant which originally came from the Amazon Rainforest of South America. The seeds are often used for coloring food.

How to use
The seeds are heated in cooking oil, usually with the proportion of 1:2 (twice as much oil as annatto seeds). Let it fry for about 5-6 minutes over medium heat or until the oil turns a reddish color. Remove from heat and let it cool off completely. Strain and discard seeds and pour into a glass container for storing.

How to store dried spices
You don't have to worry about how to store dried spices as they can last for a very long time in dried form. You just need to store them in a jar with a tight lid and be sure to avoid the heat, as the heat interacts negatively with the fragrance of the spice. You should

also avoid humidity, as too much moisture can mildew the spice.

Fruits

Like vegetables, exotic climates produce exotic fruits which are not often available fresh in other climates. I'd like to talk about them so you can have some overall ideas about what they are, so you might recognize them when you travel to Vietnam or other southeast Asian countries.

DURIAN – **sầu riêng**

Durian is considered 'king of fruits' according to southeast Asian people. It is very rich in energy and fat. It's a large fruit with sharp spikes and a very strong smell that divides eaters into two very distinctive groups. One group loves it so much, they're addicted to it; the other group finds it sickening and stays as far away from it as possible.

Durian is often eaten fresh, though it can be used for making sweet soup, sticky rice, ice cream, or cake, as it enhances the flavor for the dish with just a little scoop.

How to choose and open

The delicious durian has a greasy, savoury, sweet, and fragrant flavor, a creamy yellow color, and no grain or an imperfect grain.

Durian can come whole, peeled, or in frozen packs. If you are lucky to find peeled or frozen durian in your area, you can visualize its quality and pick a good one quite easily.

If you don't have a choice but to find a whole durian, there's a trick you can use to open it. It's really helpful in this case as durian skin is very firm and sharp, and trying to open it could hurt you, so it's helpful to know how to open it properly before buying. Additionally, it's quite risky to pick a good durian as the outside surface will be very thick.

It's necessary to choose a ripe, heavily fragrant durian because a young one is almost impossible to open and the durian meat is not sweet. A durian's smell should be strong. The outside wedges should spread out evenly and have small cracks on each wedge where, with just a little bit of effort, you can open the durian by inserting a small knife and separating the skin. Then you use two hands to open it wide and take out the wedges. Be sure the cracks are not too big and the stalk is not very dried-out; otherwise it could be too ripe, and the air coming into the durian could make it bitter.

If there are no cracks on the durian, check to see if the spikes are large, firm, not very sharp, and spread out, as this can also indicate that the durian is ripe.

Navigate to the middle of the wedge, then use a knife to cut from the top to the bottom. Use your hands to split the wedge open and remove the durian meat from each wedge. A mature durian should not be crunchy.

The seller always has a special tool to open the durian on hand. You can borrow that tool and knock on the skin to measure a durian's freshness. If you hear a sound like 'boop boop' or 'beek beek', that means the durian is mature. Avoid durians that make 'bong bong' or 'cong cong' sounds; these durians are not ripe enough to promise thick, delicious meat, and they'll often have more seeds.

How to store

Unless you are going to use the durian within a few days, I recommend freezing it to preserve its quality.

If you have peeled or packed durian, you just need to put it on a tray or plate, then wrap it in a plastic bag, squeezing out as much air as possible. If you have a lot of durian meat, keep it in a tightly closed container and put it in the freezer.

The best way to store durian is not to segment it, but to keep it whole in the freezer to preserve its fragrance, flavor, and freshness.

MANGOSTEEN – **măng cụt**

Mangosteen is a very popular exotic fruit in hot parts of Southeast Asia. In Vietnam, it is mostly grown in the south, where there is no winter. While durian is called 'The King of Fruits', mangosteen is said to be the

'Queen' due to nutritional value. It is rich in vitamins and nutrients. Its flavor is fragrant, sweet, slightly sour, and very refreshing. Mangosteen has a thick outer skin, but the white flesh inside is edible.

A good-quality mangosteen should have many wedges, with small seeds or no seeds at all, and white meat. It is often used for making sweet soups (chè), salads, cakes, and ice creams, or served fresh.

How to choose and open

It's often not easy to choose a good-quality mangosteen, even for native Vietnamese. I'll give you some suggestions, based on what we normally do when buying mangosteen:

Look at the size. A small or average-sized mangosteen, which is about the size of a small orange, is more delicious than a larger one, because it has more wedges and fewer seeds.

Look at the flower on the bottom of the mangosteen. The number of the petals reflect the number of the wedges, and the size of petals decides the size of the wedges, so it's better to pick the one that has as big and as many petals as possible. I recommend buying mangosteens with six to seven petals, if you can find them.

Look at the peel. Be sure to choose a mangosteen with a brownish peel, not a red or pink one.

Gently squeeze it. You want a mangosteen with soft skin all over.

In order to open a mangosteen, you just need to use a sharp knife to cut through half of it horizontally. Be sure not to cut too deeply into the core part, just go through the skin. Then, use your hands to halve the skin. Discard the firm outer skin of the mangosteen until you reach the inner white core, or use a fork to take out the white core part and serve.

How to store

People often store whole mangosteens, as peeled ones deteriorate easily.

Mangosteen only can last for a couple of days at room temperature. The best option for long-term storage is to store it in a fridge, where it will keep for two to three weeks. Be sure to put your mangosteen in a tightly covered plastic bag or a plastic bag with small holes before putting it in the fridge.

SNAKE FRUIT - **quả mây**

I bet many people, even southeast Asian, don't know this fruit exists. I myself only learned about it when I took a trip to An Giang Province, in western Vietnam, two years ago. Quả mây belongs to the palm family and grows in clusters. Snake fruit, like its name suggests, has a scaly, reddish-brown outer skin, like a snake with little thorns. The inside flesh is completely different; it is very smooth and milky. Snake fruit is not as soft as lychee, but it's very sweet, mildly sour, and juicy; the flavor is like a combination between pear, banana, and pineapple. Snake fruit is full of great nutrients like protein, vitamins A and C, thiamine, dietary fiber, iron, calcium, phosphorus, carbohydrates, and beta-carotene.

How to choose and open

People often choose the freshest-looking snake fruit to ensure the inside flesh won't rot too quickly. We also pick thin-skinned ones, since they're easier to open. Be sure to look at the stem; a firm stem can ensure a pleasant, crunchy flesh, which is much nicer than sponginess.

Due to its thorny skin, you have to be careful when open it to avoid scratches. Be sure to wrap the snake fruit in a thick layers of tissue paper, then open it with your fingers.

How to store

It's quite easy to store snake fruits. You just need to watch out when moving them to avoid bruising them and damaging the inside flesh.

In order to retain quality, you should keep them whole and in the fridge, where they can stay fresh for up to one week.

JACKFRUIT – **mít**

Jackfruit originally came from India, but it has become very popular nowadays in exotic regions. I'm not sure who brought it to Vietnam, or when, but jackfruit has been grown in the countryside of Vietnam for decades. Jackfruit has a tough skin with spikes. The yellowish or greenish part inside the skin, including the jackfruit's meat, fiber, and seeds, is the edible part. Jackfruit has a very sweet taste. There are different kinds of jackfruit, including Honeydew Jackfruit (mít mật), Thai Jackfruit, Seedless Jackfruit (**mít không hạt**), Tough Jackfruit (mít dai), and Artocarpus integer (mít tố nữ).

People often eat jackfruit fresh if it's ripe. Young jackfruit is often used as a vegetable in cooking soups, stir-fries, braises, or making salads. Pickled jackfruit fiber is used in salads and soups.

How to choose

As I mentioned above, there are various kinds of jackfruit. Each kind has a different flavor and texture, so serve whichever you like best.

Honeydew Jackfruit - mít mật has a tender core and a sweet, refreshing taste.

Tough Jackfruit - mít dai has a thick layer of meat, a light yellow color, a sweet and dark flavor, and a pleasant crunch.

Seedless Jackfruit - mít không hạt has a very fragrant, savory taste. The wedge and fiber are yellow, and the meat is thick with no grains. It comes with only a small amount of fiber. Over 90% of this jackfruit is edible.

Artocarpus Integer - mít tố nữ has a durian-like flavor and a stronger smell than the other types of jackfruit. Its wedges are stuck more to the core than to the skin, so when it's ripe, you can hold the stem to pull the whole wedges out of the skin easily. This is a feature special to this kind of jackfruit.

The best option for picking up your favorite kind jackfruit is to buy it packaged.

If you don't have much choice but to buy a whole jackfruit, picking the right kind is a challenge. I recommend you ask the seller directly, as it's difficult to tell jackfruits apart, since the outside skin looks quite similar among jackfruits. Only mít tố nữ can be identified with some small characteristics.

In general, for all kinds of jackfruit, the best quality will be from ripe, mature fruits. I recommend you choose a jackfruit with dark brown skin, wide spikes, a large distance between spikes. The flavor will naturally be strong and fragrant. The wedges should be yellow, and the less fiber, the better. The stem should be from 0.5 to 1 cm for mít tố nữ, and 1 to 1 ½ cm for the other jackfruits.

Jackfruit has a lot of sap, so you have to be very careful opening it, or just use your hands to eat it. To avoid the sap, use gloves, or if you don't have gloves, rubbing your hands with a little bit of cooking oil before touching the jackfruit will help. If you accidentally get some sap on your hand, you can rub your hand with a piece of lime, a handful of rice, or a dash of kerosene to remove it.

If you used a knife to open jackfruit and some sap stuck to it, put the knife in the fridge until the sap turns firm. Once it's hardened, it should be easy to discard. You also can use cooking oil or kerosene to remove the sap. Once the sap has been removed, be sure to wash your hand or knife again with warm water.

How to open

For Artocarpus Integer: Use a sharp knife to cut many lines through the skin of the jackfruit, from the top to the bottom. Then hold the stem tightly with one hand and use the other to open the skin. The yellow wedges are the edible parts, and you can use either your hand or a fork to remove them and serve.

For the other jackfruits: Hold the jackfruit horizontally. Cut it into quarters, then cut out the white part in the middle of jackfruit. Use your hand to take the edible yellowish part, then serve it. If the sap sticks to your hand or knife while you're trying to cut or serve the jackfruit, you can use a piece of newspaper to clean it up.

How to store

Unlike durian, jackfruit should be peeled and cut into wedges before storing. The best way to store jackfruit while preserving its quality is to put it in a tightly closed container or plastic bag, then store it in the fridge, where it will keep for about a week. Freezing is not suitable for storing jackfruit, as it can turn too soft when defrosting.

STARFRUIT – **khế**

Originally from Sri Lanka, starfruit has become very popular in Southeast Asia nowadays. In Vietnam, starfruit is considered a common fruit and sold at a very low price; despite how cheap it is, it brings a lot of both medical and culinary benefits. It's crunchy, delicious, and refreshing, too. Starfruit is green or yellow, and gets its name from its five wedges; when you hold the whole fruit, you can see the "star" on each half. Starfruit has a sweet and sour taste; it's also very rich in vitamin A, vitamin C, and minerals, so they are commonly used in beverages, candied fruit, soups, and stir-fries, or eaten fresh.

How to choose and open

There are two types of starfruit: sweet and sour. Sweet starfruit's wedges are often bigger and juicier than the sour kind and are often eaten fresh. Sour starfruit is normally used in cooking, or as a raw herb with bitter unripe bananas to complete the flavor of a dish. It depends entirely on your palate, so choose the starfruit that works best for you.

When buying, you should choose a fresh, juicy fruit with a recently-cut stem that sticks firmly to the fruit and as few blemishes on the outside skin as possible. You can check the freshness by using your nail to pinch the stem and looking for an oily extract coming out. Be sure to test the weight and color, because ripe starfruit should be yellow and heavy.

When serving, all you need to do is to remove the small brown seeds inside the starfruit. All other parts, including the skin, are edible.

How to store

Unless you are using starfruit within 1-2 days, you'd better keep it in the fridge. Before putting in the refrigerator, wash your starfruit under running water, then soak them in a bowl of diluted salt water for just about 5 minutes, no longer, to retain its quality. Dry them quickly and wrap cling film around each individual fruit before putting them into a tightly closed plastic bag. Be sure to squeeze out as much air as possible, then put the bag in the fridge.

Freezing is not suitable for storing fresh fruit like starfruit, as when it is brought out to room temperature, it will go bad quickly.

The best way to use fresh fruits is to purchase a small amount at a time, just enough for consuming within two days. Fruit that's been frozen or in the refrigerator is not as good as fresh fruit.

RAMBUTAN – **chôm chôm**

Chôm chôm is a tropical tree native to Southeast Asian and suitable for cultivation in non-flooding areas. Thus, rambutan in Vietnam is mainly seen in provinces in the South Central Coast, Dong Nai River Basin, and Mekong River Delta.

The edible part is the white, translucent flesh. Before serving, be sure to discard the skin and seeds. The flesh is very rich in vitamin C and iron. It has a sweet and sour flavor, and it's delicious eaten raw or in sweet soup. The name "chôm chôm" reflects the messiness of its hairs on the skin.

How to choose and open
Fresh rambutan is always highly recommended. Be sure to pick one with firm, green hair, crunchy skin, and unblemished skin. Make sure the outside isn't turning brown.

There are several kinds of rambutan:

Thai rambutan - chôm Chôm Thái is very sweet and juicy. The flesh doesn't stick to the seed. If you like to serve this, I recommend you to choose a medium-sized (about the size of a ping pong ball) rambutan with green hair and crunchy, red skin for the best quality.

Java Rambutan - chôm chôm Java has slightly sour flesh that sticks to the seed. It's dark red, and it looks bigger than other rambutans. I don't recommend this kind, as it's not as delicious as the other types.

Small Rambutan - chôm chôm Nhãn has dry, crunch, and sweet flesh that doesn't stick to the seed. The fruit is smaller than chôm chôm Thái and about half size of chôm chôm Java, with short red hair and thin red skin. It's one of the best kinds of rambutan available.

In order to reach the flesh, take a small, sharp knife and cut though the skin around the rambutan. Then use your hand to open and remove the skin. Use or serve the flesh however you'd like.

How to store

Rambutan is stored almost exactly like starfruit. Please refer to the instruction under "How to store Starfruit".

There's only one difference: it's best to store rambutan whole. If you think you might have to store part of a rambutan, be sure to use a good-quality knife when you cut through the skin, as any rust on your knife will hasten the oxidizing process of the fruit, quickly changing its color.

MOUNTAIN APPLE – **quả roi**

Roi, or Mận in the south of Vietnam, is a tropical tree widely cultivated in many Asian countries, including Vietnam itself. It's very juicy, sweet, and refreshing, with some slight sour and bitter tastes. Mountain apple provides a large amount of vitamin A, vitamin C, antioxidants, fiber, calcium, niacin, and iron. Both the skin and flesh are often eaten raw, particularly in the summer. The seeds are ground into a powder and used for making drinks.

How to choose and open
The bell-shaped mountain apple comes in a variety of sizes and colors like white, pink, red, dark red, and purple. The freshest, sweetest fruits will be heavy, firm, and fleshy. Don't buy mountain apples from a shop that regularly mists their produce, as the extra water can ruin the fruit very quickly.

You don't need any special tool to serve Roi, just rinse it well and dry it before serving. Discard the top, the bottom, any hair, and the seeds.

How to store
Mountain apple is stored exactly like starfruit. Please follow the instructions under "How to store Starfruit".

AMBARELLA - **Trái cóc**

Trái cóc has an oval shape and a lot of fibrous spikes clinging to its flesh. It is rich in protein, fiber, vitamins, and heat relieving minerals. It also helps digestion, thus helps to appetize. The flesh has sour flavor, with a small amount of sweetness, so it's particularly suitable for someone who is on a diet. It's very thick, crunchy, and refreshing, with a pineapple-esque smell. Trái cóc is commonly eaten raw or used to make drinks, salads, and candied dishes, but I think it's best when the unripe fruit is soaked in salt, sugar, chili, and shrimp paste.

How to choose and open

There are three kinds of ambarella you can find in Vietnam:

Stomach ambarella - **cóc bao tử** might be named for its use in aiding digestion, but I'm not sure. Cóc bao tử is a fruit that is harvested when it's still young. This type is small, seedless, spikeless, slightly sour, and very crunchy.

Unripe Ambarella has smooth, green skin and is firm when squeezed. I highly recommend this kind as the flesh is crunchy, slightly sour, and easy to incorporate into many dishest.

Ripe Ambarella has a bronze yellow color. The flesh is very soft, juicy, and sweeter than the unripe ambarella, so it's often eaten raw. Not many Vietnamese people fancy it.

For peeling, all you need is a sharp knife. The green flesh (for unripe ambarella) or yellow flesh (for ripe ambarella) is the edible portion. Slice the flesh lengthwise, take off each segment by hand, remove the seeds, and you are ready to serve.

How to store

Ambarella is easy to store. It can last for about 15 days if kept in the fridge. Be sure to rinse it well, dry, then put it in a plastic bag and close it tightly before putting it in the fridge. Unripe ambarella can last for long time at room temperature if you keep it whole. However, peeled ambarella should be stored in the fridge because leaving it out can turn it a blackish color.

GUAVA - ổi

Guava is one of the most popular fruits in Vietnam, and in Asia in general. Believe it or not, the guava is actually native to Brazil. It has various sizes and shapes, from 4-5 cm to as large as 9-10 cm; from round to long to pear-shaped. Guava is very rich in fiber, zinc, antioxidants, and vitamin C - even more than an orange. Ripe guava has a sour leading flavor, followed by a slightly sweet taste. Unripe guava is tart and very crunchy, so it's often used in drinks, or soaked in vinegar, sugar, salt, and chili flakes to make "sweet and sour guava". Guava can help improve your complexion, so it's popular with most ladies, and I am not an exception.

How to choose and open

There are many kinds of guava, so here's a list of the most famous varieties:

Bo Guava - ổi bo is the specialty of Vietnam's Thai Binh province. It impresses diners with its refreshing fragrance, sweet flavor, and thick, crunchy flesh with few seeds. In order to pick the right "Ổi Bo", look for a perfectly round, small to medium sized guava with a small stem and firm wedges raised above the skin's surface.

Seedless Guava - ổi không hạt seedlings are originally from Thailand. Its flavor is balanced between sour and sweet, it has no seeds at all, and the flesh is very crunchy with an appealing ivory white color. It is emerging as a favorite kind of guava in Vietnam nowadays. The seedless guava is pea-shaped, and normally bigger and longer than Ổi Bo. The average guava weight is about 400g. The skin is green and very smooth.

Queen Guava - ổi nữ hoàng is outstandingly high-quality compared to other kinds of guava, so maybe that's why it's named after the Queen. Indeed, Queen

Guava has fragrant, crunchy, white flesh, no seeds, and a well balanced sour-sweet flavor. To pick the right one, be sure to look at the outside shape. The fruit should have an oval shape, with two splints on the left side.

Gang, Dao, Mo, and Nghe Guava - ổi găng, ổi đào, ổi mỡ, ổi nghệ are grouped together due to their similarities in size, fragrance, flavor, and color. People in Vietnam prefer this group to any other type of guava, as these are super fragrant, super sweet, and very tender and juicy. Their special characteristics are small size, about half of normal size of Queen Guava; a round shape; and rougher skin.

The skin and flesh of guava are edible, but be sure to discard the seed as it has been proven to cause indigestion. Rinse your guava well before serving; you can use a knife to slice it, but my favorite way to eat guava is to just sink my teeth into the flesh. The full feeling of the flavors can be obtained this way: a little bit of bitterness, followed by a little sourness, and ending with sweetness - the taste is unforgettable!

How to store

Guava is quick to ripen. It only can stay fresh for a few days at room temperature. To retain its quality for a longer time, guava will keep in cold storage for three to four weeks. Follow the instructions under "How to store Ambarella".

Vietnam is notable for its wide variety of noodles, which can be grouped into three types: fresh, dried, or both dried and fresh. Most Vietnamese noodles are made from rice, including Bún, Bánh Đa, Phở, Bánh Hỏi, Hủ Tiếu, or Mì Quảng; while other noodles are made of wheat, like Mì Trứng and Mì ăn liền. Mì Trứng, or Egg Noodles, are a Chinese food that was introduced to Vietnam by Vietnamese Chinese people that has since become an integral part of Vietnamese cuisine. Bánh Canh is made of various ingredients including rice, tapioca flour, or wheat.

Miến, or Glass Noodles, includes products like Cellophane noodles and mung bean noodles. Recently, Vietnamese people have developed Potato and Sweet Potato Miến, and have begun using new ingredients like mushroom, seaweed, green caviar, red rice, lotus seeds, soya, and vegetable flour in other types of noodles.

Bún are the soft, round, and white rice noodles. They are the second most common noodles, with Pho being the most common. Bún is available in both dry and fresh forms, but the fresh noodles are much more popular in Vietnam. Sadly, only dry bún can be found in Western markets. Bún is used most often in noodle soups, noodle stir-fries, or served with protein, vegetables, and various dipping sauces.

Bánh Phở: Phở is Vietnam's national dish, so Bánh Phở are the most popular noodles in Vietnam. These are skinny rice noodles, slightly larger than Bún. Beside Phở, Bánh Phở is also used for stir-fries, and both deep-fried and mixed dishes.

Hủ tiếu are tough, translucent rice noodles, and a southern Vietnam special. They are available both fresh and dry; street vendors commonly use these in great noodle soups like Hủ tiếu Nam vang, Hủ tiếu Bò viên, and Hủ tiếu Mỹ tho. Hủ tiếu pairs particularly well with garlic, chives, bean sprouts, and a protein like minced pork, seafood, or beef meatballs, served with black bean sauce and chili sauce.

Bánh hỏi rice noodles are the smallest of all, and often fold in layers. They are never served with soups or stir-fries, but they're great for rolls! Together with raw vegetables, herbs and some protein, Bánh hỏi makes a perfect roll.

Miến - glass noodles go by several other names like cellophane noodles or bean threads. They are made from oriental cana or mung bean flour, and are only available in dry form. I love the texture of miến the most because they are so small, chewy, and make me feel comfortable with every bite. We make soups, salads, and stir-fries with miến, and we use them as part of the filling in spring rolls.

Mì - egg noodles are made from wheat flour, so they are quite different from common Vietnamese noodles. And yes, they originate from China. Mì comes in both dried and fresh forms, and they're often used in soups and stir-fries.

Mì Quảng is named after the province of Quang Nam in central Vietnam. These rice noodles are thick, wide, and colored yellow with turmeric. Mì Quảng can be served with or without soup and with any kind of protein, including pork, chicken, prawns, fish, or beef.

Bánh canh are the biggest and thickest noodles, compared to other types. They are made from tapioca flour or a mixture of rice and tapioca flour. As the result, they are very chewy, so we don't use them for rolls or stir-fries. Bánh canh is often available fresh and used for soups like Crab Noodle Soup and Pork Knuckle and Shrimp Soup.

Bánh đa are dry, phở-sized noodles made from rice flour, set apart from other kinds of noodles by their crunchiness. The most common form of Bánh đa is brown due to the presence of caramelized sugar. They are great for noodle soups, mixing, or stir-fries.

Mì ăn liền or instant noodles almost weren't included in this book, but at the end of the day their characteristics have convinced me. They are made from wheat flour, like many kinds of Western noodles, but they have a unique flavor that I never can overlook. I've tried many times to find out what that flavor is, what seasonings it comes from, what's in these small, thin, fragrant noodles, and what makes them so incredibly chewy, much chewier than any other type of noodles I've tried. All those features make them so deliciously distinct from other types.

Where to Buy Vietnamese Ingredients

Almost everyone who is interested in cooking Vietnamese foods will ask this question. You can look for a Chinese store, as Chinese cuisine uses many of the same ingredients. You can find Vietnamese or Chinese grocery stores anywhere there's a large Vietnamese community; I believe every country outside Vietnam should have one. You also can find some of the more exotic and authentic ingredients in places like High Street Supermarkets or World Food Counter.

For online shopping, unfortunately, there aren't many Vietnamese or Chinese shops with an online presence, and those that do tend to not accept online payment. I suggest checking out the telephone numbers of your local stores, then calling them to order and making your payment upon delivery.

Suggestions for Ingredient Substitutions

If you don't have the necessary ingredients on hand, there are substitutions you can use to help you achieve a result that's only slightly differ from the original. I'll give you a list of substitutes, but you can find a lot more on the internet. It would be hard to follow a recipe without the exact item, so I'll give you some useful tips so you can make your own substitutions. Even for cooking traditional Vietnamese dishes, you still can find most ingredients, and decent substitutions, in western countries like the UK. For example, fresh herbs, vegetables, and spices are used in many Vietnamese dishes, but I can find most of them in my area.

If I'm missing an ingredient, I'll settle on a substitute by:

Taking into account the texture, flavor, aroma, taste, moisture content, appearance, and weight of the ingredients.

For example, if I wanted to make spring rolls and I could not find jicama, I would use onion because the texture, taste, and moisture content of jicama and onion are quite similar. They are both crunchy, fragrant, sweet, watery, and white.

Chive is a good substitute for green onions.

If you can't find Vietnamese balm, you can use coriander and mint.

Seasoning powder would be a good substitute for salt, since they're both salty powders.

Fish sauce can be replaced by soy sauce because they're both liquids with a salty, umami flavor. More example would be: sugar can be substituted by healthier ingredients like honey in dipping sauce or by rock sugar in soups.

Consider the role the ingredient plays in your dish. For some unique ingredients, you may not find the perfect substitute. Look at the dish and figure out what role the ingredient plays. Then look for an ingredient that can fill a similar role. If these ingredient you're missing doesn't contribute much to the dish, I recommend you just leave it out.

For example, lemongrass has a crucial role in dipping sauces for seafood because it helps to reduce the fishy smell, but its aroma is unique. If you want to replace it, be prepared to compromise a little bit, as whatever you use to counter the fishy smell will make the dish will taste different. In this case, you should look for another ingredient that has a strong smell and works well with seafood. The substitution can be mint!

Consider the convenience, speed, and quality of the ingredients. A modern cook tends to worry about not just the quality of the food, but also time saved while cooking. In many Vietnamese recipes, including the recipes in this book, there are many ingredients that require a lot of time and energy to make. Don't worry, as modern substitutions are always available to meet your needs.

Take pork broth or chicken broth, for instance. It's believed that stock made from natural ingredients is the best option, but there are arguments that the fresh ingredients, like pork bone or chicken bone, can destroy the stock if they aren't clean, or they contain chemicals. In this case, canned stock is the perfect substitution. However, ready-made broth or concentrated stock differ from country to country, due to the use of different root vegetables and herbs. With that, I recommend you to use the unsalted type to minimize the differences. You'll have to accept that the broth will not taste exactly the same as homemade, but it still keeps its main function and flavor, which is good enough.

If you're lacking ingredients for adding aroma to the dish, an extract of that aroma is always a good substitute. It's the same with coloring: with a few drops of food coloring, you save a lot of time, and you don't have to simmer red beet or pandan leaves or other natural ingredients to bring color to the dish. However, not everyone is ok with color additives or extracts, so if you are allergic to any of them, follow the instructions under the Chapter "Vietnamese Cuisine for People with Food Restrictions and Allergies".

Vietnamese Cuisine for People with Food Restrictions and Allergies

Vegetarians

A large proportion of the Vietnamese population follows Buddhism. This is the main reason why there are so many vegetarians in Vietnam. In Vietnam, being vegetarian means no animal products and no pungent foods, but dairy products and eggs are okay. We also use tofu or seitan as protein, and add a lot of vegetables to a vegetarian meal. If you are vegetarian, the best time to go to Vietnam is in July on the lunar calendar, or about August on the Western calendar. This is Vu Lan Báo Hiếu, the month for showing gratitude to deceased parents. During this time, people tend to eat vegetarian foods, recite Buddhist sutra, and pray for spirits to move on to the next world to be reborn. All the vegetarian food is good news for you if you're also vegetarian.

On the other hand, Vietnamese food is full of hidden animal products. Fish sauce is used in almost all of our dishes, from dipping sauce to cooked food like soups, stir-fries, and grilled foods. Seasoning powder, the second most common spice in Vietnamese cooking, also comes from animal bones. There are kinds of seasoning powder for vegetarians and vegans, but they aren't as common. Shrimp paste is often used to create the characteristic flavor of numerous soups and dipping sauces. The chili paste which is served with Phở contains garlic, and garlic is considered too pungent for Vietnamese vegetarians.

Unfortunately, Vietnamese cuisine, unlike Western cuisine, often calls for sautéing pungent herbs like garlic and shallot in oil for creating a dish's aroma. Even in restaurants that sell vegan foods, they may still use garlic or shallots in their cooking and only swap out the protein, for example, swapping pork meat for tofu or vegetables. So if you pop in a restaurant, you should always keep an eye on how they make your dish. The best option is to cook at home so you have control over every ingredient. Don't forget to use the white part of a leek instead garlic or shallots if you want to be a real Vietnamese vegetarian!

Vegans

We don't have a concept of veganism in Vietnam. Fortunately, Vietnamese cooking is vegan-friendly, if you can eat pungent foods, since dairy is rare and animal products can be replaced. You can find true vegan dishes here in our country.

Lactose Intolerance

Vietnamese people, like many people in Asia, are more likely to be lactose-intolerant than people in other parts of the world. Maybe that's the reason why there's almost no dairy in our cuisine. If you're lactose-intolerant and traveling to Vietnam, you're in luck, since you won't have to worry too much about food and drinks. Most of the creamy dishes and beverages that you will see are made with coconut milk.

However, you should be careful of yoghurt, butter, sweetened condensed milk, and other milk products which are added to the more modern dishes, including cakes, crepes,and bread, that are emerging and developing all over Vietnam.

Fresh Fruit Allergies

If you cannot eat fresh fruit, then Vietnam, particularly Hanoi, is the place for you because it's a paradise of candied fruits. However, the other dishes made with cooked fruit like cake, pancakes, etc., are not part of the Vietnamese people's palate. As you may know, not every fruit can be cooked, or they may become unappetizing after cooking. If your allergy isn't too severe, you can try any fruit you like and spit out if your mouth feels itchy. The other good news is that strawberry, the fruit that causes the most allergic reactions, is not always available in Vietnam, while the other tropical fruits are massively popular.

Nut Allergies

The most common form of nut allergies is peanut allergy. Peanuts are not a kind of tree nut, but people who are allergic to peanuts can be allergic to tree nuts, as tree nuts and peanuts may come into contact during food processing. It's lucky that not many Vietnamese dishes are made from peanuts. However, there are some existing products that may use peanut or tree nuts like chili sauce, dipping sauce for summer roll, cookies, cakes, ice-cream, desserts, cooking oil made from nuts which you should stay away if you have a nut allergy. You can always look at the label before buying any product. Or the best way is to learn to cook Vietnamese food yourself! There are always non-nut substitutes for you such as sesame seeds, pumpkin seeds, sunflower seeds. Or using available medicinal herb like dried Chinese apple is a great alternative for cakes!

Fish and Shellfish Allergies
Unfortunately, it's very unlikely for a Vietnamese to be allergic to seafood as nearly all of our recipes will contain some amounts of fish sauce or seafood-based stock like shrimp paste or chili oil. Therefore, it is best advised for you to question the ingredients in advance or better yet, just stick to vegetarian dishes. Another reason for learning how to cook at home as you may know exactly what you put in your dish.

Gluten Intolerance
Well, wheat isn't popular in Vietnam at all! Our country is a paradise for you if you are sensitive to gluten. Most Vietnamese food products, like fresh fruits and vegetables, herbs, seafoods, milk products, noodles, meat products, and rice products are gluten free. However, gluten in Vietnamese food often comes hidden in some brands of soy sauce, fish sauce, and

hoisin sauce. You can always find the condiment brands that do not contain gluten, just read the labels carefully and look for the ones that are labeled 'gluten-free', or don't list 'wheat' in their ingredients.

Dishes which originate from the other parts of the world, like spaghetti, cakes, buns, etc., are more widely available in Vietnam nowadays. The batter and filling of some "Bánh," like "Bánh xèo," "Bánh gối," "Bánh Khọt," "Bánh Khoái," and noodles called Mỳ should also be avoided if you have celiac disease.

Special dishes

Cuisine is different from country to country. Some ingredients which are rare or even taboo in other countries are commonly used in Vietnam and considered some of the best sources of protein for the human body.

Here's my list of the top ten uncommon dishes:

Balut - hột vịt lộn is underdeveloped duck egg. If you travel to Vietnam, you'll see balut sold almost everywhere. It has savory, fatty taste, and it's very nutritious and rich in vitamin A. The way Vietnamese eat balut is different from other countries in Asia, as we serve it with Vietnamese coriander (**rau răm**) and ginger to cut the "coldness" of balut.

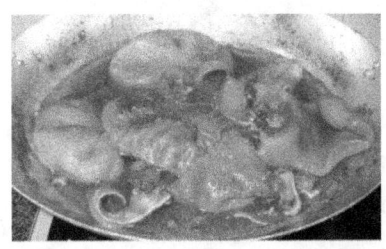

Organ Meat Stew - phá lấu is made from the organs and meat of animals, most commonly pork and beef. Don't panic, all the ingredients are rinsed clean before cooking. Phá lấu is a super delicious, full of nutrients, and often served with Bánh Mì.

Snail & Crab Noodle Soup - bún riêu ốc is a popular street food in Vietnam. As you can tell from its name, bún riêu ốc has paddy crab and paddy snails as the main ingredients. Its typical taste comes from the sourness of fermented rice and fermented shrimp, the aroma of perilla, the crunchiness of crab, and the savory taste of snail.

Fresh Ragworm   Ragworm Pancake

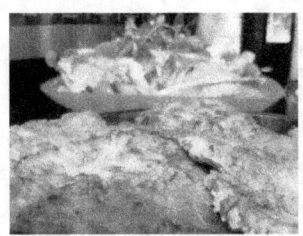

Dipped Ragworms - chả rươi is a northern Vietnamese specialty, made with ragworm, sometimes called "Earth Dragon". Chả rươi is seasonal favorite that appears from about October to December every year. The harmonious, sophisticated combination of flavors and ingredients like ragworm, minced pork, eggs, green onions, an tangerine peel in this dish can make it irresistible.

Fried Bees - ong chiên are a specialty of the mountainous regions of Vietnam. At first glance, you might feel horrible due to its appearance, but if you have the courage to take a bite, you will ask for another, as this dish is very umami, savory, and chewy. It works especially well with alcohol.

Sauté Silkworm with Lime Leaves - nhộng rang lá chanh are very nutritious, as silkworms are very rich in protein, vitamins, amino acids, and lipids. Toast silkworms with lime leaves to make a very nutty-tasting dish.

Duck Blood Pudding - tiết canh vịt is another dish that might make you feel weird or scared, due to its name and the appearance of fresh blood! I put it here because tiết canh is a unique traditional dish among world cuisines. Drinkers in Vietnam particularly like this food, as the finishing dish has the balanced flavor of duck meat, blood, and fresh herbs and vegetables.

Dried Pancake with Millet - bánh đa kê is one of my favorite street foods from childhood. The freshness of millet, the savory taste of mung beans, together with the crispiness of dried pancake...wow, I never can forget its delicious flavor, even though I haven't eaten it for almost twenty years! I am sure you will also fall in love with this common dish when you try it.

Sticky rice with Ant Eggs - xôi trứng kiến is the specialty of a minority group in northern Vietnam called the **Tày**. Ant eggs are only available from April to May, and they're very expensive, but worth the cost. Served on a plate of fragrant sticky rice with crispy fried shallots and umami spices, the ant eggs will burst "blip, blip" in your mouth while chewing, making an unforgettable impression.

Bull Penis - ngẩu pín is one of the strangest dishes for foreigners. Bull penis, like other animal parts that are often disposed of in many Western countries, is considered a precious ingredient in Vietnamese cooking as it helps to enhance a man's libido.

Vietnamese cuisine is also notable for its wide range of uncommon meats. Some of these meats are dog, cat, rat, snake, crocodile, squid, deer, porcupine, and goat. When cooked, these are transformed into numerous dishes including barbecues, stir-fries, soups, or braised dishes. It's believed that these sources of protein are much richer than other common meats.

Many of the traditional Lunar New Year dishes such as Jellied Pork Jelly – **Thịt đông (recipe in Part 2),** Pig Head Sausage – **Giò thủ,** and Pig Skin Soup – **Canh măng móng giò** involve the use of pig heads, tongues, throats, feet and skin. For example, Pig Skin Soup is made with pig skin that's been baked until it popped.

Other animal parts used in Vietnamese cooking include beef tails; chicken heads, necks, and feet; and pork bones, where the most umami stocks come from.

However, one must say that not all traditional dishes are good and deserve to be preserved like cuisine heritage of a nation. Eating cat which catch mice thus protect human crops or eating freshly drawn blood - **tiết canh** are not welcomed nowadays.

Cooking Utensils

I would like to bring this topic up just to get you acquainted with popular Vietnamese tools and equipment. You don't need special utensils for your cooking; since its inception, Vietnamese cuisine has used chopsticks for almost every one of our recipes, from stir-fries, to deep-fries, to soups and more. A common cooking set only consists of chopsticks and six other things: a skillet, a saucepan, a knife, a cutting board, a strainer, and a ladle. With these, our ancestors created and developed so many delicious dishes.

If all you have are your favorite or heavily-used utensils, you can still cook most Vietnamese foods. However, the dream kitchen of every family should be equipped with several other tools that make your cooking more convenient. You should pick these tools according to your interests. I prefer using a mortar and pestle for grinding over a cutting board and knife, and I'd rather use a wok for stir-frying than a skillet. I also like using a steamer instead a of rice cooker for sticky rice.

Traditional Lunar New Year dishes

Typical Dishes for Vietnamese Tet: Left to right: Vietnamese Pork Sausage (Giò lụa), Trưng Cakes (Bánh Trưng), Dried Candied Fruits (Mứt), Pickled Small Leeks (Củ kiệu), Dried Shrimp (Tôm khô)

Tet, or Lunar New Year, is the most important celebration of the year for Vietnamese people. It is not only the time for people to welcome the New Year with the hope of receiving good things in upcoming year, but also the best time to come back home, have a family reunion, and enjoy Tet's delicious traditional dishes in the warm atmosphere.

There are similarities in the Tet's Feast Tray among the three main regions of Vietnam (the North, South, and Middle); long grain rice, broken rice, sticky rice, Chung Cake (Bánh Chưng), Cylindrical Sticky Rice Cake (Bánh Tét), and Pickles are compulsory components. But due to the difference in climate, location, and customs, there are typical features of cuisine in each region in Vietnam.

Tet in the North
The Tet's Feast Tray in Northern Vietnam has four bowls and plates symbolizing the year, month, day, and hour; the four directions; or the four seasons of the year. A bigger tray should have six or eight sets of bowls and plates, to symbolize luck and wealth according, to oriental perspectives.
The four bowls include Pig Knuckle and Bamboo Shoot Soup (Canh móng giò hầm măng), Pig Skin Soup (Canh bóng thả), Glass Noodle Soup with Chicken Breast (Canh miến gà), and Pork Paste and Mushroom Soup (Canh mọc nấm thả). Additionally, there are families who prepare more soups made of birds, chicken, abalone or shark fin.
The four plates should include Chopped Boiled Chicken (Gà luộc), Chopped Boiled Pork (Thịt lợn luộc), and Roasted Cinnamon Pork (Chả quế), Pork Sausage (Giò lụa), Pig Head Sausage (Giò thủ). Some families also add a plate of Jellied Pork (Thịt đông), Spring Rolls (Nem), Mix Stir-fry (Xào thập cẩm), Salad Kohlrabi (Nộm su hào), or Celery (Cần tây) to their tray.

Tet in Central Vietnam

Central Vietnam suffers through a lot of severe weather conditions, so the constant failure of crops result in a lack of many fresh ingredients. However, the coastline around central Vietnam is long, and known for its salt and fish sauce industries.

Therefore, food is prepared with the salty, bold flavors of the sea, so they can preserve their food for a long time.

In central Vietnam, all the dishes in the tray are divided into small plates or bowls, a few at a time, and put on a round tray as a way of showing thrift and sharing.

The most common dishes are Rice (Cơm), Boiled Chicken (Gà luộc), Boiled Pork (Heo luộc), Beef Sausage with White Pepper (Giò bò tiêu sọ), Pickled Shrimp (Tôm chua), Cylindrical Sticky Rice Cake (Bánh Tét), Fried Eggs (Trứng chiên), Mixed Stir-fry (Xào thập cẩm), Braised Pork (Thịt kho), Simmered Shrimp (Tôm rim), Pork Soaked in Fish Sauce (Thịt heo ngâm nước mắm),

Stir-Fry Meat and Dried Bamboo Shoot (Thịt xào măng khô), Chicken Salad with Vienamese Mint (Gỏi gà rau răm), Squid Salad (Gỏi mực), Figs Salad (Gỏi vả), Fermented Pork Rolls (Nem chua), and Pork Skin Rolls (Nem bì-(tré). You can also find several kinds of wraps and rolls, including boiled or braised Pork Rolls and Fish Rolls.

Tet in Southern Vietnam

With the pleasant weather, the lack of large storms and cold weather, and the proximity to the Mekong Delta, Southern Vietnam has a lot of fresh ingredients, including different kinds of fish, that open the door to producing a wide variety of Mắm. Cá lóc, **cá linh** and a wide range of tropical fruit like mangosteen, mango, and dragon fruit are easy to find. The southern diet is very 'green', with vegetables, fish, and tropical fruits as the main ingredients. Thus, the traditional Southern Vietnamese meal has more diverse and richly-flavored dishes than other parts of the country.

During Tet, the rice tray offered to the ancestors commonly has Caramelized Pork with Eggs (Thịt kho trứng) to serve with Pickled Bean Sprouts, Stuffed Bitter Melon Soup (Canh khổ qua nhồi thịt), and Cylindrical Sticky Rice Cake (Bánh Tét). Apart from that, there are indispensable dishes such as Lotus Stem Salad (Gỏi Ngó sen), Pickled Pig Ears (Tai heo ngâm dấm), Dried Shrimp – Pickled Small Leeks (Tôm khô – Củ kiệu), Phá lấu, Fermented Pork Rolls (Nem chua), Spring Rolls (version of southern Vietnamese and Stuffed Pork Leg (Chân giò nhồi). The amazing dessert that closes the meal is Fermented Glutinous Rice (Cơm rượu/Rượu nếp).

Dried Candied Fruits (Mứt tết) is an indispensable dish of traditional Vietnamese Tet throughout all regions of Vietnam. In every family there is a tray of Mứt tết together with roasted pumpkin or watermelon seeds and a teapot with cups. "Mứt" is made from all sorts of fruits and vegetables, including apples, banana, coconuts, persimmons, breadfruit, carrots, tomatoes, squash, ginger, peanut, calamondin, courgette, and lotus seeds.

Making Mứt is simple, but time-consuming, so it requires some patience. First, the raw materials are cleaned and peeled, then soaked in sugar. This step often takes at least 2-3 hours, or you could soak your ingredients overnight. Then, cook your ingredients on low heat for several hours until all the water evaporates. Some types of Mứt have the sticky consistency of jam. Some varieties, like Peanut (lạc) are covered with a thick layer of sugar, but most have only a thin layer of sugar.

Vietnamese add color to Mứt by using natural ingredients. For example, to get a red color we use beetroot, a green color is taken from pandan leaves, yellow from gardenia seeds, purple from magenta plant, and coconut milk contributes to a white color.

Part 2

Introduction

In Vietnam, the food is just as important as the culture itself. When people often think of Vietnam, they often think of the poverty stricken families first, instead of learning that what makes this people rich is their love for the food that is passed down through the generations. When teaching members of the family how to cook, it is typically done by passing down stories of the cooking process.

While I can't tell you a story to help you cook authentic Vietnamese food, I can show you how to make some of the most popular Vietnamese dishes for yourself. While it may be hard to find a few of the herbs that you need as some are only native to Vietnam, by the end of this book you will learn how to properly prepare authentic Vietnamese food completely from scratch. With the help of over 25 Vietnamese recipes, I know you will become a Vietnamese chef in no time!

So, let's stop wasting time and get to cooking!

Rice Vermicelli With Chicken

This is a dish that uses a condiment that is typically used in crunchy noodle salads. In this particular dish, it helps to give it the perfect combination of sweet and spicy flavor.

Makes: 4 servings

Total Prep Time: 50 minutes

Ingredients:
- 1 ½ pounds of chicken breasts, skin on and bone-in
- Dash of salt
- 1 shallot, thinly sliced
- ½ cup of vegetable oil
- 8 ounces of rice vermicelli noodles
- 1 Fresno chile, seeds removed and chopped
- 1 clove of garlic, grated
- 1/3 cup of lime juice
- ¼ cup of fish sauce
- 2 Tbsp. of light brown sugar
- 4 baby white turnips, thinly sliced
- 4 radishes, trimmed and thinly sliced

- 1 ½ cups of Thai basil leaves, evenly divided

Directions:

1. Preheat an outdoor grill to medium heat.

2. Season the chicken with a dash of salt. Place onto the preheated grill. Cook for 20 to 25 minutes or until the chicken is cooked through. Transfer the chicken onto a plate. Set aside to cool completely. Shred the chicken off of the bone. Toss out the bones.

3. In a saucepan set over medium heat, add in the vegetable oil. Add in the sliced shallot. Cook for 8 to 10 minutes or until golden. Transfer onto a plate and season with a dash of salt.

4. Place the noodles into a boil. Cover with boiling water. Soak for 5 to 10 minutes or until soft. Rinse the noodles and drain.

5. In a separate bowl, add in the chopped Fresno chile, lime juice, fish sauce and light brown sugar. Stir well to mix. Add in the soft noodles, sliced white turnips, sliced radishes, half of the chopped Thai basil leaves and shredded chicken. Stir well to mix. Toss well to mix.

6. Serve with the remaining Thai basil leaves garnished over the top.

Vietnamese Lemongrass Curry Chicken

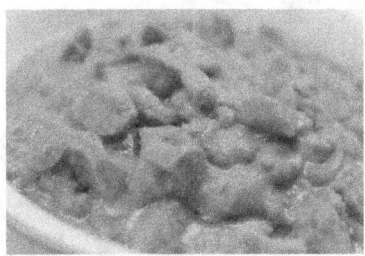

This recipe was actually passed down from my family and now I want to pass it down to you. It is one of the most aromatic and spicy curry dish that you can make.

Makes: 4 servings

Total Prep Time: 40 minutes

Ingredients:
- 2 Tbsp. of vegetable oil
- 1 lemongrass, minced
- 1, 3 pound whole chicken, cut into pieces
- 2/3 cup of water
- 1 Tbsp. of fish sauce
- 1 ½ Tbsp. of powdered curry
- 1 Tbsp. of cornstarch
- 1 Tbsp. of cilantro, chopped

Directions:

1. In a skillet set over medium heat, add in the vegetable oil. Add in the minced lemongrass. Cook for 5 minutes or until fragrant.

2. Add the chicken into the skillet. Cook for 10 minutes or until the chicken is cooked through.

3. Add in the water, fish sauce and powdered curry. Increase the heat to high. Allow to come to a boil. Lower the heat to low and cook for 10 to 15 minutes at a simmer.

4. In a bowl, add in the cornstarch and 2 tablespoons of curry sauce. Stir well until smooth in consistency. Pour into the skillet. Continue to cook for 5 minutes or until thick in consistency.

5. Remove from heat. Serve immediately with a garnish of chopped cilantro.

Beef Meatball Pho

This is a delicious pho dish you can make whenever you need something extremely filling. One bite and I know you will become hooked.

Makes: 12 servings

Total Prep Time: 5 hours and 45 minutes

Ingredients:
- 1 pound of beef steak, cut into cubes
- 1 Tbsp. of fish sauce
- 1 tsp. of potato starch
- ¼ sp. of baker's style baking soda
- 2 Tbsp. of ice water
- 1 Tbsp. of garlic, minced
- 1 tsp. of black pepper
- Vegetable oil, for greasing
- Dash of salt

Ingredients for the pho:
- 2 ½ Tbsp. of salt, evenly divided
- 4, 2 inch pieces of ginger, smashed

- 2 ½ pounds of beef marrow bones
- 1 ½ pound of beef shank
- 5 shallots
- 2 star anise
- 1 black cardamom pod
- 1, 2 inch stick of cinnamon
- ¼ cup of fish sauce
- 14 ounces of dried pho noodles, cooked
- 1 pound of beef tenderloin, thinly sliced
- 8 scallions, chopped
- 1 cup of cilantro leaves, chopped
- 1 lime, cut into wedges and for serving
- Hot chile slices, for serving
- Dash of black pepper

Directions:

1. In a Ziploc bag, add in the beef shank cubes. Seal the bag and place into the freezer to freeze for 2 hours.

2. In a bowl, add in the fish sauce, potato starch and baker's style baking soda. Stir well to mix. Transfer into a food processor. Add in the ice water. Pulse on the highest setting. Transfer back into a bowl.

3. In the bowl, add in the beef cubes and toss well to mix. Season with a dash of salt and black pepper.

4. Grind the beef mixture until paste like in consistency.

5. Brush a plate with vegetable oil. Shape the beef mix into balls and roll in the vegetable oil.

6. In a saucepan set over medium to high heat, add in the meatballs. Over with water and season with a dash of salt. Allow to come to a boil. Lower the heat to low. Cover and cook for 10 minutes. Transfer the meatballs onto a plate and set aside.

7. Prepare the pho. In a stockpot, fill with water and season with a dash of salt. Add in the smashed ginger, beef marrow bones and beef shank. Soak for 1 to 2 minutes. Drain. Place the bones and beef shank back into the pot.

8. Pour in water to cover. Set over high heat and allow to come to a boil. Drain and rinse the bones and beef.

9. In a saucepan set over high heat, add in the star anise, black cardamom and stick of cinnamon. Cook for 1 to 2 minutes or until fragrant. Transfer into a tea bag

and add into the stockpot. In the stockpot, add in the shallots and ginger pieces.

10. Add in 8 cups of water into the stockpot. Allow to come to a boil over high heat. Lower the heat to low and cook for 1 hour. Remove the beef shank and set aside to cool. Continue to cook for 1 hour.

11. Remove the ball of spices and continue to cook at a simmer for 2 hours. Season with a dash of salt and the fish sauce.

12. Slice the beef shank into slices.

13. Prepare the pho noodles according to the directions on the package. Once cooked, transfer the pho noodles into serving bowls.

14. Pour the broth over the noodles. Top off with the sliced beef shank and meatballs.

15. Serve immediately.

Vietnamese Grilled Snapper

This delicious snapper dish is made using a turmeric marinade that helps to give this dish a unique and earth flavor that everybody will love.

Makes: 6 servings

Total Prep Time: 4 hours and 15 minutes

Ingredients:
- 4 cloves of garlic, thinly sliced
- 2 Tbsp. of turmeric, chopped
- ½ tsp. of salt
- 1 shallot, chopped
- 4 scallions, chopped
- 1 Fresno chile, chopped
- 1 jalapeno pepper, seeds removed and chopped
- 1 Tbsp. od lemongrass, chopped
- 3 Tbsp. of white sugar
- ¼ cup of lime juice
- 1 Tbsp. of fish sauce
- 6, 4 ounce snapper, skin-on

- 12 turmeric leaves, extra for serving
- White rice, cooked and for serving
- Lime wedges, for serving

Directions:

1. With a mortar and pestle, add in the sliced garlic, chopped turmeric and dash of salt. Pound until coarse in consistency. Transfer into a bowl.

2. In the bowl, add in the chopped shallots, chopped scallions, chopped Fresno chile, chopped lemongrass, white sugar, lime juice, fish sauce and water. Stir well until evenly mixed.

3. Season the snapper with a dash of salt. Add into the marinade and toss well to coat.

4. Cover and place into the fridge to chill for 4 hours.

5. Preheat a grill to medium or high heat.

6. Place the marinate snapper between two turmeric leaves. Place onto the grill and grill for 5 minutes on each side or until cooked through.

7. Remove from the grill. Serve immediately with the rice and lime wedges.

Crispy Vietnamese And Pancakes

These hot and filled crepes are a popular breakfast dish served in Vietnam. With one bite, you can bring the heart of Vietnam into your own home.

Makes: 4 servings

Total Prep Time: 25 minutes

Ingredients for the batter:
- 1 cup of rice flour
- ½ tsp. of powdered turmeric
- ½ tsp. of salt

Ingredients for Assembly:
- 5 Tbsp. of vegetable oil, evenly divided
- 4 ounces of shrimp, peeled and deveined
- Dash of salt and black pepper
- 6 scallions, thinly sliced
- 4 ounces of mung bean sprouts
- Bibb lettuce leaves, for serving

Directions:

1. In a bowl, add in the rice flour, powdered turmeric, dash of salt and 1 ½ cups of water. Stir well until mixed. Cover and set aside to rest for 1 hour.

2. In a skillet set over medium to high heat, add in 1 tablespoon of vegetable oil. Add in the shrimp. Season with a dash of salt and black pepper. Cook for 3 minutes or until bright pink. Transfer onto a plate and set aside.

3. Clean the skillet. Add in the remaining 4 tablespoons of vegetable oil. Pour ½ cup of the batter into the skillet. Swirl the skillet around to swirl the batter around. Cook for 4 minutes.

4. Top off with ¼ of the sliced scallions, ¼ of the bean sprouts and ¼ of the cooked shrimp. Flip and continue to cook for another 3 minutes or until crispy. Transfer onto a plate.

5. Repeat.

6. Serve while hot.

Vietnamese Summer Rolls

If you love the taste of traditional spring rolls, then these are rolls that I know you will fall in love with. Made with plenty of veggies and packed full of an authentic Vietnamese flavor I know you won't be able to get enough of.

Makes: 12 servings

Total Prep Time: 15 minutes

Ingredients:
- 1 tsp. of white sugar
- 1 Tbsp. of lime juice
- 1 Tbsp. of mirin
- 1 Tbsp. of soy sauce
- 1 Tbsp. of rice vinegar
- 2 ounces of rice noodles, thin
- 12, 8 inch rice paper rounds
- 2 cups of Bibb lettuce leaves, cut into halves
- 1 cup of rotisserie chicken, shredded
- 1 red bell pepper, thinly sliced
- 1 carrot, thinly sliced

- 1 Persian cucumber, thinly sliced
- ½ of an avocado, thinly sliced
- 1 red chile, optional
- ½ cup of cilantro leaves, chopped
- ½ cup of mint leaves, chopped

Directions:

1. In a bowl, add in the white sugar and 1 tablespoon of water. Stir well until the sugar dissolves. Add in the lime juice, mirin, soy sauce and rice vinegar. Stir well to mix and set the sauce aside.

2. Prepare the rice noodles according to the directions on the package. Drain the noodles and set aside.

3. Dip the rice papers into warm water and place onto a flat surface.

4. Add ½ of a Bibb lettuce leaf into the center of each rice paper. Top off with the rice noodles, shredded rotisserie chicken, chopped red bell pepper, chopped carrot, chopped cucumber and avocado. Finish off with a topping of the red chiles, chopped cilantro leaves and chopped mint leaves.

5. Fold the rice paper over the filling and roll like a burrito. Cut in half and place onto a serving plate.

6. Serve immediately with the dipping sauce.

Vietnamese Pork Chops

When making these pork chops, make sure to go light on the seasoning. Either way I know you will love these pork chops.

Makes: 4 servings

Total Prep Time: 50 minutes

Ingredients:
- 1 shallot, chopped
- 1/3 cup of light brown sugar
- ¼ cup of fish sauce
- 2 Tbsp. of unseasoned rice vinegar
- 1 tsp. of black pepper
- 4, 1 inch thick pork chops, bone-in
- 1 Tbsp. of vegetable oil
- Dash of salt
- Lime halves, for serving

Directions:

1. In a shallow dish, add in the chopped shallot, light brown sugar, fish sauce, rice vinegar and dash of black pepper. Whisk well to mix.

2. Pierce the pork chops with a fork. Transfer into the marinade. Toss gently to coat.

3. Cover and set aside to marinate for 20 minutes.

4. Remove the pork chops from the marinade.

5. In a skillet set over medium to high heat, add in the vegetable oil. Add in the pork chops. Season with a dash of salt. Cook for 5 minutes on each side or until browned. Remove and set aside to rest for 10 minutes.

6. Pour the marinade into a saucepan set over medium heat. Allow to come to a boil. Cook for 5 minutes or until reduced.

7. Serve the pork chops with a drizzling of the marinade and lime halves over the top.

Vietnamese Vegetarian Curry Soup

This is the perfect soup dish for you to make whenever you are feeling under the weather or whenever you are craving something on the spicy side.

Makes: 8 servings

Total Prep Time: 2 hours

Ingredients:
- 2 Tbsp. of vegetable oil
- 1 onion, chopped
- 2 shallots, thinly sliced
- 2 cloves of garlic, chopped
- 1, 2 inch piece of ginger root, thinly sliced
- 1 stalk of lemongrass, cut into 2 pieces
- 4 Tbsp. of powdered curry
- 1 green bell pepper, chopped
- 2 carrots, peeled and thinly sliced
- 8 mushrooms, thinly sliced
- 1 pound of fried tofu, cut into pieces
- 4 cups of vegetable broth
- 4 cups of water

- 2 Tbsp. of vegetarian fish sauce, optional
- 2 tsp. of crushed red pepper flakes
- 1 bay leaf
- 2 kaffir lime leaves
- 8 potatoes, cut into quarters
- 1, 14 ounce can of coconut milk
- 2 cups of bean sprouts, for garnish
- 8 sprigs of cilantro, chopped and for garnish

Directions:

1. In a stockpot set over medium heat, add in the vegetable oil. Add in the onion and shallots. Cook for 5 minutes or until soft.

2. Add in the garlic, ginger, minced lemongrass and powdered curry. Continue to cook for 2 minutes.

3. Add in the green bell pepper, chopped carrots, chopped mushrooms and fried tofu pieces. Stir well to mix.

4. Pour in the vegetable stock and water. Season with fish sauce and the crushed red pepper flakes. Allow to come to a boil.

5. Add in the potatoes and can of coconut milk. Allow to come back to a boil. Lower the heat to low. Cook for 40 minutes to 1 hour or until the potatoes are soft.

6. Remove from heat.

7. Serve with a garnish of bean sprouts and chopped cilantro.

Vietnamese Braised Pork With Noodles

This is the epitome of Vietnamese cuisine that every member of your family will love. It is versatile, every one of your guests can customize their own bowl.

Makes: 6 servings

Total Prep Time: 5 hours

Ingredients for the pork:
- 2 shallots, chopped
- 2 stalks of lemongrass, chopped
- 2 Tbsp. of low sodium soy sauce
- 1 Tbsp. of fish sauce
- 1 Tbsp. of hot chili paste
- 2 tsp. of salt
- 2 tsp. of white sugar
- 1 ½ tsp. of powdered Chinese five spice
- 1 pound of pork shoulder, boneless and cut into halves
- 1 pound of pork belly, skin-on and cut into halves
- 2 Tbsp. of vegetable oil
- 6 cloves of garlic, chopped

Ingredients for the noodles:
- ½ cup + 1 Tbsp. of vegetable oil
- 4 wonton wrappers, cut into squares
- Dash of salt
- 1 pound of dried and wide rice noodles
- 8 ounces of mung bean sprouts
- 1 Fresno chile, thinly sliced
- 1 lime, cut into wedges
- Hot chili paste, for serving

Directions:

1. Prepare the pork. In a bowl, add in the chopped shallots, chopped lemongrass, soy sauce, fish sauce, hot chili paste, white sugar, powdered five spice and dash of salt. Stir well to mix. Add in the pork shoulder and belly. Toss well to mix.

2. Cover and set into the fridge to chill for 3 hours.

3. Remove the pork from the marinade. Set the marinade aside.

4. In a Dutch oven set over medium to high heat, add in 2 tablespoons of vegetable oil. Add in the pork. Cook for 10 to 15 minutes or until browned. Remove and transfer onto a plate.

5. In the Dutch oven, add in the garlic. Cook for 1 minute. Add in the marinade and 4 cups of water. Allow to come to a boil.

6. Add in the pork. Lower the heat to low. Allow to come to a simmer. Cook for 1 ½ hours. Remove and set aside to cool.

7. Prepare the noodles. In a skillet set over medium to high heat, add in ½ cup of vegetable oil. Add in the wonton wrappers. Fry for 3 minutes or until golden brown. Transfer onto a plate lined with paper towels. Season with a dash of salt.

8. Prepare the wide rice noodles according to the directions on the package. Once cooked, transfer to a colander. Add in 1 tablespoon of vegetable and toss well until coated.

9. Remove the pork from the liquid and slice into slices that are ¼ inch in thickness.

10. Bring the pork liquid to a boil. Add in ½ cup of water. Lower the heat to low. Season with a dash of salt. Cook for 5 minutes. Remove from heat. Add in the sliced pork and set aside to cool.

11. Add the noodles back into boiling water for 30 seconds. Drain and transfer onto a plate. In the same pot, add in the bean sprouts and cook for 30 seconds. Drain and place on top of the noodles.

12. Ladle the pork and cooking liquid over the noodles.

13. Serve the noodles and pork with chile, lime wedges, wontons, sliced chile, hot chile paste and lime wedges.

Roasted Shrimp Sausage Rolls

This is a traditional Vietnamese dish that is typically grilled for street dishes. It is perfect to make during your next family barbecue.

Makes: 10 servings

Total Prep Time: 45 minutes

Ingredients:
- Vegetable oil, for greasing
- 1 egg white
- 1 Tbsp. of fish sauce
- 1 tsp. of cornstarch
- ¼ tsp. of black pepper
- 1 pound of shrimp, peeled and deveined
- 1 shallot
- 1 Tbsp. of honey
- 1 cup of mint leaves
- 1 head of lettuce

Directions:

1. Preheat the oven to 450 degrees. Place a sheet of aluminum foil onto a baking sheet. Grease with vegetable oil.

2. In a bowl, add in the egg white, fish sauce, cornstarch and black pepper. Transfer this mix into a food processor.

3. In the food processor, add in the shrimp and shallot. Pulse 6 times for at least 10 seconds or until paste like in consistency.

4. Divide the paste into 10 portions. Form the portions into sausage shapes and place onto the baking sheet. Brush the sausages with a tablespoon of vegetable oil.

5. Place into the oven to bake for 20 minutes.

6. Increase the oven to a broil.

7. Brush the honey over the sausages. Broil in the oven to 3 to 5 minutes.

8. Remove the sausages from the oven. Wrap in mint and lettuce leaves. Serve.

Vietnamese Long Bean Salad

This is a light and savory salad dish you can serve whenever you are craving something on the lighter side. Feel free to top this salad with whatever toppings you wish.

Makes: 4 servings

Total Prep Time: 15 minutes

Ingredients:
- ½ cup of unsweetened coconut flakes
- 1 bunch of watercress, cut into 2 inch lengths
- Dash of salt
- ¾ pound of Chinese long beans
- 2 Tbsp. of fish sauce
- 2 Tbsp. of lime juice
- 1 Tbsp. of coconut sugar
- ½ of a red onion, thinly sliced
- 1 Tbsp. of kaffir lime leaves, thinly sliced
- ¼ cup of roasted peanuts, chopped

Directions:

1. Preheat the oven to 350 degrees.

2. In a baking sheet, add in the coconut flakes. Place into the oven and bake for 5 minutes or until golden. Remove and set aside to cool completely.

3. In a saucepan set over medium heat, add in the watercress and cover with salted water. Allow to come to a boil. Transfer into a colander and drain.

4. Return the saucepan over medium heat and allow to come to a boil. Add in the Chinese long beans. Cook for 5 minutes or until soft. Transfer into an ice bath. Drain and pat dry with a few paper towels.

5. In a bowl, add in the fish sauce, lime juice and coconut sugar. Whisk until the sugar dissolves.

6. In the bowl, add in the watercress, Chinese long beans, thinly red onion and sliced kaffir lime leaves. Toss well to coat.

7. Serve with a topping of the toasted coconut flakes and chopped roasted peanuts.

Shrimp And Mango Salad

This is a light and tasty salad dish you can make whenever you are craving something on the sweeter side. Be sure to use the freshest mango for the tastiest results.

Makes: 2 servings

Total Prep Time: 30 minutes

Ingredients:

- 1 tsp. of salt
- 1 pound of shrimp
- 1 mango, peeled, pits removed and shredded
- 1, 2 inch piece of ginger, peeled and minced
- ½ cup of mint leaves, chopped
- ½ cup of roasted peanuts, chopped

Ingredients for the salad dressing:

- 2 ½ Tbsp. of lime juice
- 2 Tbsp. of fish sauce
- 3 Tbsp. of white sugar
- 1 Tbsp. of garlic, minced

- 1 ½ tsp. of hot chile, minced

Directions:

1. Fill a saucepan with water. Add in the salt and allow to come to a boil over high heat. Add in the shrimp. Cover and allow to come back to a boil. Remove the cover and continue to cook for an additional 2 minutes.

2. Transfer the shrimp into a bowl filled with ice water.

3. Peel the shrimp.

4. In a bowl, add in the peeled shrimp, chopped mango and ginger. Toss well to mix.

5. Prepare the dressing. In a bowl, add in all of the ingredients for the dressing. Whisk well until the sugar fully dissolves. Pour over the salad and toss well to coat.

6. Serve the salad with a garnish of peanuts and mint leaves.

Vietnamese Grilled Lemongrass Shrimp And Noodles

This is the perfect noodle recipe you can make whenever you have a craving for shrimp. Packed with an authentic Vietnamese flavor I know you will love.

Makes: 6 servings

Total Prep Time: 15 minutes

Ingredients:
- 1 pound of shrimp, peeled and deveined
- ½ of a stalk of lemongrass, chopped
- 1 Fresno chile, seed and chopped
- 2 cloves of garlic, chopped
- 1 tsp. of salt
- 1 tsp. of white sugar
- 8 ounces of vermicelli noodles
- Vegetable oil, for greasing
- ½ of a cucumber, peeled and cut into thin strips
- 1 carrot, peeled and sliced into thin strips
- ¼ cup of peanuts, roasted and chopped

- Sprigs of cilantro, chopped and for serving

Directions:

1. In a bowl, add in the deveined shrimp, chopped lemongrass, chopped garlic, chopped Fresno chile, dash of salt and white sugar. Stir well to mix. Cover and place into the fridge to chill for 1 hour.

2. Prepare the vermicelli noodles according to the directions on the package. Transfer the noodles into a colander and set aside.

3. Prepare an outdoor grill to medium or high heat. Grease the grated of the grill with vegetable oil. Add in the shrimp and grill for 2 minutes or until cooked through.

4. Transfer the shrimp onto a serving plate.

5. Top off with the cucumber, carrot strips, chopped peanuts, chopped cilantro, shallots and cooked noodles.

6. Serve.

Caramel Catfish

While caramel and seafood doesn't seem like an appetizing combination, you will be pleasantly surprised the moment you get a taste of it.

Makes: 4 servings

Total Prep Time: 45 minutes

Ingredients:
- 1/3 cup of water
- 2 Tbsp. of fish sauce
- 2 shallots, chopped
- 4 cloves of garlic, minced
- 1 ½ tsp. of black pepper
- ¼ tsp. of crushed red pepper flakes
- 1/3 cup of water
- 1/3 cup of white sugar
- 2 pounds of catfish fillets
- ½ tsp. of white sugar
- 1 Tbsp. of lime juice
- 1 green onion, thinly sliced

- ½ cup of cilantro, chopped

Directions:

1. In a bowl, add in 1/3 cup of water and fish sauce. Stir well to mix.

2. In a separate bowl, add in the shallots, minced garlic, dash of black pepper and crushed red pepper flakes. Stir well to mix and set aside.

3. In a skillet set over medium heat, add in 1/3 cup of water and 1/3 cup of white sugar. Stir well to mix. Cook for 3 minutes or until the sugar is golden brown.

4. Add in the fish sauce mix and allow to come to a boil. Add in the shallot mix. Add in the catfish. Cover and cook for 5 minutes on each side or until the catfish is cooked through.

5. Transfer the catfish onto a plate and set aside.

6. Increase the heat to high. Add in ½ teaspoon of white sugar and lime juice. Allow to come to a boil. Lower the heat to low and cook for 3 minutes or until the sauce has been reduced. Remove from heat.

7. Pour the sauce over the catfish.

8. Serve the catfish with a garnish of green onions and chopped cilantro.

Green Papaya Salad

This is another delicious salad dish that is highly popular throughout various parts around Vietnam. It is made with a natural sweetness that compliments any dish that you may make.

Makes: 2 servings

Total Prep Time: 30 minutes

Ingredients:

- ½ of a green papaya, peeled, seeds removed and shredded
- 1 carrot, peeled and shredded
- 1 tsp. of salt
- ½ cup of mint leaves, chopped
- ½ cup of Vietnamese balm leaves, chopped
- ½ cup of roasted peanuts, chopped

Ingredients for the dressing:

- 2 ½ Tbsp. of lime juice
- 2 Tbsp. of fish sauce
- 3 Tbsp. of white sugar
- 1 Tbsp. of garlic, minced

- 1 ½ tsp. of hot chile, minced

Directions:

1. Prepare the dressing. In a bowl, add in all of the ingredients for the dressing. Stir well to mix. Set the dressing aside.

2. In a bowl, add in the shredded green papaya, shredded carrot and dash of salt. Stir well to mix. Set aside to rest for 10 minutes.

3. Rinse out the papaya mixture under running water. Drain the mix and squeeze out the excess water. Place the mix back into the bowl.

4. Dressing the mix over the top. Toss well to coat.

5. Add in the chopped mint, chopped cilantro and balm leaves. Toss well to mix.

6. Place the salad onto a plate.

7. Serve with a topping of the chopped peanuts.

Chicken Papaya Salad

This is a spicy salad that you can make whenever you are craving something exotic. It is a bit on the sweet side so it should satisfy those picky eaters in your home.

Makes: 6 servings

Total Prep Time: 20 minutes

Ingredients for the chicken:

- 4 chicken breasts, skinless and boneless
- 1 Tbsp. of low sodium soy sauce
- 1 tsp. of sugar
- ¼ tsp. of powdered Chinese five spice
- Dash of salt and black pepper
- Vegetable oil, for greasing

Ingredients for the salad:

- 2 cloves of garlic, chopped
- 2 Tbsp. of lime juice
- 2 tsp. of white sugar
- 1 tsp. of fish sauce

- ½ of a green papaya, cut julienne style
- ½ of a cucumber, peeled and cut julienne style
- 1 daikon, peeled and cut julienne style
- 1 carrot, peeled and cut julienne style
- 6 scallions, sliced julienne style
- 1 Fresno chile, chopped
- Dash of salt and black pepper
- 2 Tbsp. of toasted sesame seeds

Directions:

1. Prepare the chicken. In a bowl, add in the chicken. Add in the soy sauce, white sugar, powdered Chinese five spice, dash of salt and black pepper. Stir well to mix. Cover and set aside to rest for 1 hour.

2. Prepare a grill to medium or high heat. Grease the grate of the grill with vegetable oil.

3. Add the chicken onto the grill. Cook for 5 to 8 minutes or until the chicken is cooked through. Remove and set aside to cool before shredding.

4. Prepare the salad. In a bowl, add in the chopped garlic, lime juice, white sugar and fish sauce. Whisk until evenly mixed. Add in the cooked grilled chicken.

5. Add in the papaya, sliced cucumber, sliced daikon, chopped carrot, sliced scallions and chopped Fresno chile. Toss well to mix.

6. Season with a dash of salt and black pepper.

7. Serve the salad with a garnish of the toasted sesame seeds.

Vietnamese Butternut Squash And Salmon Porridge

This is a dish that contains two Vietnamese favorites such as butternut squash and pumpkin. Made with natural sweetness, this is a dish that can help to satisfy your strongest sweet tooth.

Makes: 4 servings

Total Prep Time: 1 hour and 10 minutes

Ingredients:
- 4 ¼ cups of chicken stock
- 1 ½ cups of butternut squash, cut into cubes
- ¼ cup of jasmine rice
- ¼ cup of glutinous rice
- 1 Tbsp. of salt
- 2 pounds of salmon fillet, cut into cubes
- 3 Tbsp. of soy sauce
- 1 tsp. of black pepper
- 3 Tbsp. of vegetable oil
- 5 scallions, chopped and parts separated

- Dash of black pepper

Directions:

1. In a saucepan set over medium to high heat, add in the chicken stock. Allow to come to a boil.

2. Add in the butternut squash cubes and jasmine rice. Allow to come to a boil. Lower the heat to low. Cook for 15 minutes. Turn off the heat and cover. Set the pan aside to rest for 15 minutes. Season with a dash of salt.

3. Season the salmon with a dash of black pepper and soy sauce.

4. In a saucepan set over high heat, add in the vegetable oil. Add in the white parts of the scallions. Cook for 30 seconds. Add in the salmon cubes and cook for an additional 2 minutes or until the salmon is browned.

5. Ladle the porridge into bowls. Top off with the salmon and scallion greens.

6. Season with a dash of black pepper. Top off with shallots.

7. Serve immediately.

Vietnamese Thit Bo Xao Dau

This is a wonderful Vietnamese dish you can mix whenever you are craving authentic stir fry. It is made with hearty beef and green beans to make a hearty and healthy dish you can make any night of the week.

Makes: 4 servings

Total Prep Time: 30 minutes

Ingredients:

- 1 clove of garlic, minced
- ¼ tsp. of black pepper
- 1 tsp. of cornstarch
- 1 tsp. of vegetable oil
- 1 pound of sirloin tips, thinly sliced
- 3 Tbsp. of vegetable oil
- ½ of an onion, thinly sliced
- 2 cups of green beans, trimmed
- ¼ cup of chicken broth
- 1 tsp. of soy sauce

Directions:

1. In a bowl, add in the minced garlic, dash of black pepper, cornstarch and 1 teaspoon of vegetable oil. Stir well to mix. Add in the beef and stir well to mix.

2. In a wok set over high heat, add in 2 tablespoons of vegetable oil. Add in the mixed beef and cook for 2 minutes or until the beef begins to turn brown. Transfer onto a bowl and set aside.

3. In a wok, add in the remaining tablespoon of vegetable oil. Add in the onion and cook for 5 minutes or until soft.

4. Add in the green beans and chicken broth. Cover and lower the heat to medium. Continue to cook at a simmer for 5 minutes or until the green beans are tender.

5. Add in the soy sauce and the cooked beef. Toss well to mix. Cook for 1 to 2 minutes.

6. Remove from heat and serve immediately.

Vietnamese Saigon Chicken Salad

This is another great tasting salad dish that you can make whenever you need something more on the healthier side.

Makes: 4 servings

Total Prep Time: 3 hours and 25 minutes

Ingredients for the chicken:
- 1 cup of cilantro, chopped
- 5 Tbsp. of lemon juice
- 1, 4 inch pieced of lemongrass, chopped
- 3 kaffir lime leaves, minced
- ½ cup of extra virgin olive oil
- Dash of salt
- 1 ¼ pounds of chicken breast, boneless, skinless and cut into halves

Ingredients for the dressing:
- 5 Tbsp. of fish sauce
- ¼ cup of gold brown sugar
- ¼ cup of lime juice

- 2 tsp. of Thai chiles, minced
- 2 cloves of garlic, pressed

Ingredients for the vegetables:
- 3 cup of Chinese long beans, sliced into 2 inch pieces
- 8 ounces of plum tomatoes, cut into halves and thinly sliced
- 1 cup of daikon, peeled and grated
- 1 cup of Persian cucumbers, seeds removed and grated
- 1 cup of green cabbage, thinly sliced
- 1 cup of carrot, grated
- 1 cup of celery leaves
- 1 cup of cilantro leaves, chopped
- 3 green onions, thinly sliced
- ½ cup of roasted peanuts, split in halves

Directions:

1. Prepare the chicken. In a bowl, add in the chopped cilantro, lemon juice, chopped lemongrass and minced kaffir lime leaves. Stir well to mix.

2. Add in the extra virgin olive oil. Season with a dash of salt and black pepper.

3. Place the chicken breasts into a baking dish. Pour the marinade over the top. Toss the chicken lightly to coat. Cover and place into the fridge to chill for 3 hours.

4. In a skillet set over medium to high heat, add ion the chicken and ¼ cup of the marinade. Cook for 5 minutes on each side or until cooked through. Turn off the heat of the skillet and set aside to rest for 15 minutes.

5. Transfer the chicken onto a flat surface and slice into thin strips.

6. Prepare the dressing. In a bowl, add in the fish sauce, sugar, lime juice, minced Thai chiles and pressed garlic. Whisk well until the sugar dissolves. Season with a dash of salt and black pepper. Cover and set aside to rest.

7. Prepare the vegetables. In a saucepan filled with boiling water, add in the Chinese long beans. Cook for 3 minutes or until crispy. Drain the beans and set aside.

8. Transfer the beans into a bowl. Add in the sliced plum tomatoes, grated daikon, grated cucumbers, sliced green cabbage, grated carrot, chopped cilantro, sliced green onions and the peanuts. Toss well to mix.

9. Add in the chicken slices and dressing. Toss well to mix. Season with a dash of salt and black pepper. Toss again to mix.

10. Serve with a sprinkling of extra peanuts.

Rib Bun Soup

This particular soup recipe is perfect to make during the breakfast or lunch and is popular through parts of north Vietnam.

Makes: 3 or 4 servings

Total Prep Time: 1 hour and 10 minutes

Ingredients:

- 2 Tbsp. of salt, evenly divided
- 3 pounds of ribs, cut into small pieces
- 1 onion, cut into halves
- 1 ½ pounds of taro root, peeled and thinly sliced
- 4 ¼ cups of water
- 3 Tbsp. of fish sauce, evenly divided
- 1 tsp. of powdered turmeric
- 1 ½ tsp. of black pepper
- 3 Tbsp. of vegetable oil, evenly divided
- 3 Tbsp. of shallot, minced
- 6 scallions, cut into pieces and separated
- 1 ½ pounds of tomatoes, peeled and sliced into wedges

- 10 ounces of rice vermicelli, cooked
- 1 cup of Thai basil, chopped
- Cilantro leaves, chopped and for garnish
- Hot chili sauce, for serving

Directions:

1. In a saucepan set over high heat, add in 1 tablespoon of salt and fill with water. Allow to come to a boil. Add in the ribs and allow to come back to a boil. Drain the ribs and rinse under water. Clean out the saucepan.

2. Pour 4 ¼ cups of water into the saucepan. Add in the rinsed ribs and onion. Allow to come back to a boil over high heat. Reduce the heat to low and simmer for 1 hour.

3. In a colander, add in ½ a tablespoon of salt over the taro root. Squeeze the excess moisture for 3 minutes. Rinse under running water. Set the taro aside.

4. Transfer the ribs into a bowl. Set the rib stock aside. Season the ribs with 1 tablespoon of fish sauce, powdered turmeric and dash of black pepper.

5. In a saucepan set over high heat, add in 2 tablespoon of vegetable oil. Add in the shallot and cook for 30 seconds. Lower the heat to medium and add in the ribs. Continue to fry for 3 minutes. Transfer into a bowl.

6. In the same saucepan set over high heat, add in 1 tablespoon of vegetable oil. Add in the white scallions. Cook for 1 minute or until golden. Add in the tomatoes and dash of salt. Cook for 5 minutes. Remove from heat.

7. Add the tomato mix into the rib bone broth. Set over medium to high heat and allow to come to a boil. Add

in the taro root and allow to come back to a boil. Season with 2 tablespoons of fish sauce.

8. Add the vermicelli noodles into serving bowl. Top off with the ribs, scallion greens, chopped basil and chopped cilantro. Pour the stock over the top.

9. Serve immediately with a garnish of hot chili sauce.

Vietnamese Fried Chicken Thighs

If you love the taste of traditional fried chicken, then this is the perfect dish for you. It is packed with an authentic Vietnamese taste that will help to make it stand out.

Makes: 4 servings

Total Prep Time: 2 hour and 35 minutes

Ingredients:
- 8 chicken thighs, skin-on and bone-in
- 2 Tbsp. of low sodium soy sauce
- Vegetable oil, for frying
- ¾ cup of rice flour
- 1 shallot, chopped
- 2 cloves of garlic, chopped
- 1 Tbsp. of ginger, peeled and chopped
- 2 Tbsp. of light brown sugar
- ½ tsp. of salt
- ½ tsp. of black pepper
- 3 Tbsp. of fish sauce
- 3 Tbsp. of hot chili paste

- 2 Tbsp. of lime juice
- Lime wedges, for serving

Directions:

1. In a bowl, add in the chicken thighs and soy sauce. Cover and set into the fridge to chill for 1 hour.
2. In a skillet set over medium to high heat, add in 1 inch of vegetable oil. Heat the oil to 350 degrees.
3. In a bowl, add in the rice flour. Dredge the chicken in the flour and place immediately in the vegetable oil. Fry the chicken for 10 to 12 minutes or until the chicken is cooked through. Transfer onto a plate and set aside to cool for 10 minutes.
4. In a skillet set over medium to high heat, add in 3 tablespoons of the frying oil. Add in the chopped shallot, chopped garlic and chopped ginger. Stir well to mix. Cook for 3 minutes or until soft.
5. Add in the light brown sugar and two tablespoons of water. Season with a dash of salt and black pepper. Cook for 3 minutes or until foamy in consistency. Add in the fish sauce and cook for an additional 2 minutes.
6. Add in the hot chili sauce and lime juice. Stir well to incorporate.
7. Brush the chicken with the glaze.
8. Serve with a garnish of lime wedges and extra glaze.

Vietnamese Gold Chicken Wings

These are fantastic wings that are perfect for practically any occasion. Perfect for weeknight dinners or parties, this dish is packed with a Vietnamese flavor your guests will love.

Makes: 4 servings

Total Prep Time: 2 hours and 45 minutes

Ingredients:
- 12 chicken wings, tips removed and wings cut
- 2 cloves of garlic, peeled and chopped
- ½ of an onion, thinly sliced
- ¼ cup of soy sauce
- ¼ cup of Asian fish sauce
- 2 Tbsp. of lemon juice
- 2 Tbsp. of sesame oil
- 1 tsp. of salt
- 1 tsp. of black pepper
- 1 Tbsp. of powdered garlic
- 1 Tbsp. of white sugar

Directions:

1. In a bowl, add the chicken wings, chopped garlic and sliced onion. Stir well to mix.

2. Add in the soy sauce, fish sauce, lemon juice and sesame oil. Season with powdered garlic, white sugar, dash of salt and black pepper. Toss well until coated.

3. Cover and place into the fridge to chill for 2 hours.

4. Preheat the oven to 400 degrees. In a baking dish, add a sheet of aluminum foil.

5. Remove the chicken wings from the marinade. Place into the baking dish.

6. Place into the oven to bake for 30 minutes or until golden.

7. Remove and rest for 5 minutes before serving.

Vietnamese Chicken Noodle Soup

This is the perfect Vietnamese dish that you can make whenever you are feeling under the weather. It is incredibly easy to make, making it perfect for those with various cooking experiences.

Makes: 6 servings

Total Prep Time: 3 hours

Ingredients for the chicken stock:
- 1, 3 ½ to 4 pound chicken
- 1 onion, peeled and cut into halves
- 2 carrots, peeled and cut into 1 inch pieces
- 1 stalk of celery, cut into 1 inch pieces

Ingredients for the soup:
- 2 pounds of chicken legs, bone-in and skin-on
- ¼ tsp. of powdered Chinese five spice
- 1 tsp. of grated ginger, peeled and cut into halves
- 1 Tbsp. of salt
- 1 Tbsp. of white sugar
- 2 onions, peeled and cut into halves

- 2, 6 inch pieces of lemongrass, smashed
- 6 black cardamom pods, crushed
- 4 whole star anise pods
- 2 sticks of cinnamon
- 6 cloves, whole
- 1 Tbsp. of fish sauce
- 1 pound of wide rice noodles
- 8 ounces of mung bean sprouts
- Cilantro, chopped and for serving
- Lime wedges, for serving

Directions:

1. Prepare the chicken stock. In a pot set over medium to high heat, add in the chicken, chopped onion, carrots, chopped celery and 5 quarts of water. Allow to come to a boil. Lower the heat to low and cook for 2 hours.

2. Strain the stock through a mesh sieve into a bowl. Toss out the solids. Set aside to cool completely. Cover and place into the fridge to chill.

3. Season the chicken legs with the powdered five spice, grated ginger, dash of salt and 1 tablespoon of sugar. Set aside to rest for 15 minutes.

4. Preheat the oven to broil.

5. On a baking sheet, add half of the ginger and chopped onion. Place into the oven to broil for 15 to 20 minutes. Add the lemongrass, cardamom pods, star anise, cinnamon sticks and whole loves to the baking sheet. Place back into the oven to broil for 1 minute or until charred slightly.

6. Transfer the onion mix into a pot. In the pot, add in the chicken stock and fish sauce. Allow to come to a boil.

7. Add in the seasoned chicken. Lower the heat to low. Cook for 20 to 25 minutes.

8. Transfer the chicken onto a plate. Set aside to cool slightly before removing the meat from the bones.

9. Continue to cook the broth for 1 hour or until it slightly reduces. Season with a dash of salt and black pepper. Strain the broth into a bowl.

10. Prepare the noodles according to the directions on the package. Drain in a colander and place into serving bowls.

11. Top the noodles with the shredded chicken and bean sprouts. Pour the hot broth over the noodles.

12. Serve with a topping of the chopped cilantro and lime wedges.

Pineapple Shrimp Banh Mi

This is a modern Vietnamese dish that everybody will fall in love with. It is made with a pineapple sauce that gives this dish even more of a unique flavor.

Makes: 3 servings

Total Prep Time: 25 minutes

Ingredients for the shrimp:
- 1 pound of shrimp, peeled and deveined
- 2 Tbsp. of shallot, minced and evenly divided
- 2 Tbsp. of fish sauce
- 1 tsp. of black pepper
- ½ tsp. of white sugar
- 4 Tbsp. of vegetable oil and evenly divided
- 1 Tbsp. of garlic, minced
- 1 cup of pineapple, chopped
- 1 Tbsp. of hot chile, minced
- 1 tsp. of salt

Ingredients for the banh mi:
- 3 Vietnamese baguettes, cut into thirds
- ½ cup pf cilantro, chopped

- ½ cup of mint leaves, chopped

Directions:

1. Prepare the shrimp. In a bowl, add in the shrimp, 1 tablespoon of shallots, fish sauce, dash of black pepper and the white sugar. Stir well to mix.

2. In a saucepan set over high heat, add in 2 tablespoons of vegetable oil. Add in the garlic. Cook for 1 minute or until fragrant. Lower the heat to medium. Add in the chopped pineapple, minced hot chile and dash of salt. Cook for an additional 2 minutes.

3. In a saucepan set over medium to high heat, add in 2 tablespoons of vegetable oil. Add in 1 tablespoon of shallots. Cook for 1 minute or until fragrant.

4. Lower the heat to medium. Add in the shrimp. Cook for 5 minutes or until the shrimp turns brown.

5. Add in the pineapple mix and continue to cook for 3 minutes. Toss well to mix.

6. Remove from heat.

7. Slice the baguettes and spread the pineapple sauce over both sides. Top off the shrimp, chopped mint and chopped cilantro.

8. Serve.

Stir Fried Beef Bun Salad

This is a southern Vietnamese style salad dish that is highly popular in Vietnamese homes today. Made with fresh vegetables and savory beef, this is a salad you don't have to feel guilty about enjoying.

Makes: 2 servings

Total Prep Time: 25 minutes

Ingredients:
- 8 ounces of beef tenderloin, thinly sliced
- 3 Tbsp. of vegetable oil, evenly divided
- 1 ½ Tbsp. of soy sauce
- 1 ½ tsp. of black pepper
- 2 Tbsp. of garlic, minced
- 7 ounces of rice vermicelli, cooked
- 1 cucumber, shredded
- 1 carrot, shredded
- 1 cup of Thai basil leaves, chopped
- 1 cup of cilantro leaves, chopped
- 1 cup of mint leaves, chopped

- 1 cup of roasted peanuts, chopped

Directions:

1. Season the sliced beef with 1 tablespoon of vegetable oil and a dash of black pepper.

2. In a skillet set over high heat, add in 2 tablespoons of vegetable oil. Add in the minced garlic. Cook for 30 seconds. Add in the seasoned black pepper. Cook for 2 minutes or until browned.

3. In a bowl, add in the cooked vermicelli, shredded cucumber, shredded carrot, chopped Thai basil leaves, chopped cilantro, chopped mint and the chopped peanuts. Toss well to mix.

4. Add in the beef and toss again.

5. Serve the salad immediately.

Conclusion

Well, there you have it!

Hopefully by the end of this book you have found plenty of authentic Vietnamese recipes that you can make from the comfort of your own home. By the end of this cookbook, not only do I hope you have learned how to properly make homemade Vietnamese recipes from scratch but have also discovered a few new recipes you can make along the way.

So, what is next for you?

The next step for you to take is to begin making all of the recipes you have found inside of this book. Once you have done that, it will be time for you to try to find even more Vietnamese recipes that you can make in your home.

Good luck!

www.ingramcontent.com/pod-product-compliance
Lightning Source LLC
Chambersburg PA
CBHW071441070526
44578CB00001B/183